DEBORAH KOENKER

Grapes and Tortillas

Contents

Because we have a heart that sings rancheras and feet that polka

Executive Director's Acknowledgements

The Kelowna Art Gallery is pleased to present the exhibition *Deborah Koenker: Grapes and Tortillas*, along with this publication, showcasing the work of this senior Vancouver-based artist. This show examines the conditions facing the Mexican temporary agricultural workers who come to the Okanagan to work in the orchards and vineyards.

On behalf of the Board of Directors and staff, I would like to thank Koenker for her thoughtful, informative and sensitive exhibition. Thanks to our curator, Liz Wylie, for her enthusiasm and rigour realizing the exhibition, this publication, and for her thoughtful and informative essay, *Crossing Over: The Art of Deborah Koenker*. In addition, we are honoured and grateful to include texts by Juan Felipe Herrera, Randy Lee Cutler, and John Vaillant.

As always, thanks to all Kelowna Art Gallery staff, who work collaboratively to realize important projects such as this one. We are grateful to Kyle L. Poirier, our graphic designer, for his creative work on this catalogue.

As always, we are deeply indebted to all our supporters, members, volunteers, and sponsors for their continued support of our exhibitions, publications and public programs. The assistance of the City of Kelowna, the Canada Council for the Arts, the British Columbia Arts Council, the Province of British Columbia, School District # 23 and the Regional District of Central Okanagan allows us to bring important exhibitions and publications such as this one to fruition. Their ongoing support is very much appreciated.

– Nataley Nagy, Executive Director

Introduction

By Liz Wylie

Working with Deborah Koenker on this project has been an eye-opening journey. I first met Koenker about twenty years ago, but we did not discuss an exhibition until I began work at the Kelowna Art Gallery nine years ago. The idea of trying to meet and talk with the temporary agricultural workers placed here in the Okanagan came to her about four years ago, and we both went into full research mode, ably and kindly assisted by her husband, Roberto Pacheco, who originally hails from Mexico. Koenker has been tireless in her travels up and down the Okanagan Valley talking with both the Mexican workers and those individuals who have support roles for them. I had not realized before that there were over 2000 of these men and women in the Okanagan every year, so I did not know either the terms under which they come here. This information will be set out in the texts that follow in this publication.

Koenker's approach to her photographs allows these 160 people to speak directly to us – the viewers of her show and readers of this publication. Each sitter states in such open, direct, and honest terms their thoughts about being here, as they have written them with markers on a tortilla, and held it up to her camera to be photographed along with his or her own face. Koenker has translated these texts into English, and they appear alongside the reproductions of each sitter's image in this book.

In addition to her work making up the multi-faceted installation that the exhibition has become in her hands, we have produced this publication, and I am very pleased to have included such important texts by well-known and gifted writers. John Vaillant is an award-winning Vancouver-based writer, whose first novel *The Jaguar's Children* (2015) gives readers a chilling portrait of life in contemporary (post NAFTA) Oaxaca in Mexico. His text here provides his point of view and skill as a writer who can evoke, time, place and mood. Juan Felipe Herrera is currently the poet laureate of the US. We are honoured to have a short text from him about his decision to compose his poem *187 REASONS MEXICANOS CAN'T CROSS THE BORDER*, and are most grateful to him for permission to print the entire poem here. Vancouver-based Randy Lee Cutler explores the topic of the true cost of the food we buy and eat. The curatorial text on Deborah Koenker's art by myself is meant to provide a context for this project, both in art historical terms, and within the trajectory of her artistic career.

Certain experiences in our lives are so intense as to crack open our minds to new information and ideas. We call these life-changing, and I must say that the work on this project and all I have learned along the way, has been that for me. I am deeply grateful.

GENOVEVA
6 AÑOS TRABAJANDO
EN OLIVER, PUEBLO MUY
BELLO DE CANADA.
DESEO QUE MI FAMILIA
VENGA ALGUNA VEZ A VISI-
TARME.
PROPONGO QUE EL GO-
BIERNO NOS DE OPORTU-
NIDAD DE QUE NUESTROS
HIJOS ESTUDIEN EN
CANADA.

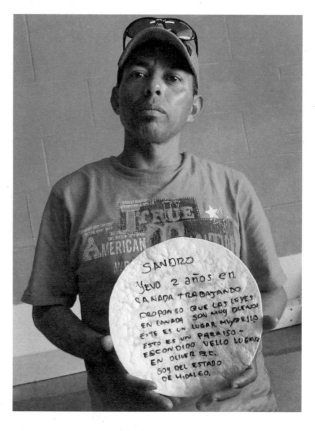

SANDRO
YEVO 2 años en
CANADA TRABAJANDO
PROPONGO QUE LAS LEYES
EN CANADA SON MUY BUENAS
ESTE ES UN LUGAR MUY BELLO
ESCONDIDO VELLO LUGAR
EN OLIVER B.C.
SOY DEL ESTADO
DE HIDALGO.

Carlos
bueno MI deseo
Es Realmente hacer
algo en Mexico hacer
algo por MI Familia Y Realmente
Por ellos Estoy haci Para
Sacarlos Adelante y tener
una Mejor calidad de
Vida

Soy de chihuahua
PARRAL
Tengo 3 años biniendo
Y Me a gustado venir
Y poder Ayudar a mi
FAMILIA Y poder
demostrar a
venimos A trabajar
FRANCISCO.G
Montes.J

6

01. Genovéva Acosta Netro, San Luis Potosi

Genovéva 6 años trabajando en Oliver, pueblo muy bello de Canada. Deseo que mi familia benga alguna vez a visitarme. Propongo que el govierno nos de oportunidad de que nuestros hijos estudien en Canadá.

Genovéva (Genevieve) 6 years working in Oliver, a very beautiful town in Canada. I wish that my family could come to visit me sometime. I propose that the government give us the opportunity that our children study in Canada.

02. Sandro

Yevo 2 años en Canadá trabajando. Propongo que las leyes en Canadá son muy buenos. Este es un lugar muy bello. Esto es un paraiso— Escondido vello lugar en Oliver B.C. Soy del Estado de Hidalgo.

I've been working 2 years in Canada. I suggest that the laws in Canada are very good. This is a very beautiful place. It is a paradise—a hidden beautiful place in Oliver B.C. I am from the state of Hidalgo.

03. Carlos Cabrera, Colima

Carlos. bueno mi deseo es realmente hacer algo en México hacer algo por mi familia y realmente por ellos estoy aqui para sacarlos adelante y tener una major calidad de vida.

Carlos. Well my desire is actually to make something in Mexico, to make something for my family and actually it's for them I 'm here, to bring them up and to have a better quality of life.

04. Francisco J. Montes G., Parral, Chihuahua

Soy de Chihuahua Parral. Tengo 3 años biniendo y me a gustado venir y poder ayudar a mi familia y poder demostrar q venimos a trabajar Francisco J. Montes G.

I am from Chihuahua Parral. I have come for 3 years and I have liked to come and to be able to help my family and to be able to show that we come to work. Francisco J. Montes G.

Soy Sergio
Me gustaría toer
a mi Familia
con migo y así
Salir adelante

― Soy de Tamoulips

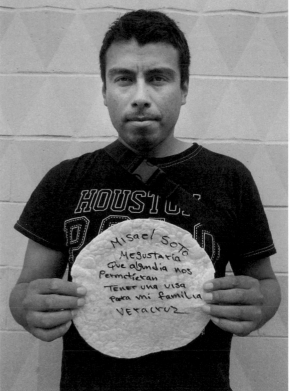

Manuel Domínguez
Esperamos que algún día
se nos tomarámos en cuenta
como buenos trabajadores
y aun más como personas
que estamos sacando adelanta
los trabajos pesados y cansados de este país.
Gracias

Soy Alfredo
Me vine d canda
Por que quiero Progresar
Y sacar adelante a
mi familia

Misael Soto
Megustaría
Que algundia nos
Permitieran
Tener una visa
Para mi familia
VERACRUZ

05. Manuel Domínguez

*Manuel Dominguez. Esperamos que algun
dia se nos tomaramas en cuenta como buenos
trabajadores y aun más como personas que
estamos sacando adelante los trabajos pesados y
cansados de esto pais Gracias*

Manuel Dominguez. We hope that someday
they take note that we are good workers
and even more as people that are pulling
forward with the heavy and tiring work of
this country. Thank you.

06. Sergio, Tamaoulipas

*Soy Sergio me gustaria taer a mi familia con
migo y asi salir adelante   Soy de Tamaoulipas.*

I am Sergio. I would like to bring my family
with me and to move forward. I am from
Tamaoulipas.

07. Alfredo

*Soy Alfredo me vine a Canda por que quiero
progresar y sacar adelante a mi familia.*

I am Alfredo. I came to Canada because
I want to progress and pull my family
forward.

08. Misael Soto, Veracruz

*Misael Soto Me gustaria que algun dia nos
permiteran tener una visa para mi familia.
Veracruz.*

Misael Soto. I would like that someday
they allow us to have a visa for my family.
Veracruz.

"MIGUEL
ANGEL CONTRERAS"
LLEVO SEIS AÑOS EN CANADA Y ME
GUSTA MUCHO, ES UN PAIS TRANQUILO
Y RESPETUOSO.
PERO PIDO AL GOBIERNO QUE NOS OTORGE
VISAS A NUESTRA FAMILIA PARA QUE NOS PUEDAN
VISITAR POR LO MENOS UNA VEZ POR TEMPORADA

TAMBIEN PIDO A LA GOBERNADORA DE BRITISH
COLUMBIA, QUE VALORISA A LOS TRABAJADORES AGRICOLAS
PORQUE GRACIAS A NOSOTROS LAS FARMAS ESTAN
SUPERANTO CADA DIA Y QUEREMOS QUE NOS
PAGUEN LOS DIAS FESTIVOS

JULIAN del estado de cununimjunto
Yo Pienso que cualple es justo
Yo quiero que Los canarios no nos Mi
Ren como vichos Raros
Porque todos somos Igualos
I estoy Agusto en
Pantixtco

Mexico — Canada
Me gustan sus bonitos
paisajes y sobre todo su tranquilidad. Qué nos quitaron menos
impuestos el gobierno Y nos apoyara
mas para imerar mas ingresos economicos
para nuestra Familia. Y sobre todo mas
apoyo cuando un compañero se
encuentra enfermo.
Ubaldo Ramirez Blancas
Estado De Mexico

Eligio Sosa Perez
Estado de Puebla
Me gustaria mas apoyo del
gobierno de nuestras necesidades
Y me gustaria que nos pudiera
Visitar algun familiar aqui
en la granja

10

09. Miguel Angel Contreras, San Juan Yutla, Oaxaca

"Miguel Angel Contreras" Llevo seis años en Canadá y me a gustado mucho, es un pais tranquilo y respetuoso. Pero pido al gobierno que nos otorque visas a nuetra familia para que nos pueden visitar por lo meno una vez por temporada. Tambien pido a la bobernadora de British Columbia, que volorisa a los trabajadores agricolas porque gracias a nosotros las farmas estan superánto cada dia y queremos que nos paguen los dias festivas.

"Miguel Angel Contreras" I have 6 years in Canada and I have liked it a lot, it is a quiet and respectful country. But I ask that the government issue our families visas to allow them to visit for at least once per season. Also I ask that the Premier of British Columbia should appreciate the agricultural workers because thanks to us the farms are improving daily and we want them to pay us for holidays.

10. Julian, Irapuato, Estado de Guanajuato

Julian del Estado de Guanajuato Yo pienso que Canadá es vonito yo quiero que los Canarios no nos miren como vichos rarros porque todos emos iguales I estoy agusto en Pentinton

Julian from the state of Guanajuato. I think that Canada is pretty and I want Canadians not to look at us like "strange insects" (weirdos) because we are all equal. I am happy in Penticton.

11. Ubaldo Ramirez Blancas, Otumba, Estado de México

Mexico – Canada Me gustan sus bonitos paisajes y sobre todo su tranquilidad. Qué nos quitaran menos impuestos el govierno y nos apoyara mas para jenerar mas ingresos economicos para nuestra familia. Y sobre todo mas apoyo cuando un compañero se encuentra enfermo. Ubaldo Ramirez Blancas Estado de México

Mexico – Canada
I like its pretty landscapes and especially its tranquility. (I wish) that the government would deduct less taxes and that the government would support us to generate more economic income for our family. And above all more support when a coworker becomes sick.   Ubaldo Ramirez Blancas, State of Mexico.

12. Eligio Sosa Perez, Zacatlán, Puebla

Me gustaria mas apoyo del gobierno de nuestras necesidades y me gustaria que nos pudeiran visitar algun familiar aqui en la granja

I would like more support from the government for our necessities and I would like that our families would be able to visit here on the farm.

13. Sergio Aguilera, Chihuahua

Sergio Aguilera Keremos K el gobierno de Canadá de permisos de k pueda benir la familia con nosotros los travajadores agricolas Soy de Chihuahua.

Sergio Aguilera We would like that the government of Canada allow our family to come with us, the agricultural workers. I am from Chihuahua.

14. Santos Jimenéz Goméz, Chiapas

Mi nombre es Santos Jimenéz Gómez vengo del Estado de Chiapa y llo pienso que en Canadá es bonito y taquilo pero tambien el sueo esta muy bajo y tambien que nos permitan con la familia y estoy trabajando en queremeos.

My name is Santos Jimenéz Gómez. I come from the state of Chiapas and I think that Canada is pretty and peaceful but also the pay is very low, and also that they allow (us to come) with the family; and I am working in Keremeos.

15. Ifren Cuevas, Veracruz

Soy Ifren Cuevas este es el segundo año biniendo a Canadá y la verdad es bonito trabajar en este pais por atraves de el estoy sacando a mi falia adelante Pero lo que no me gusta son los Patrones indianos por que ellos nos discriminan y tambien nos dan malas viviviendas para vivir y nos quieren ber mas bajo que ellos en este pais balemas lo mismo no importa de que pais eres Estado Veracruz

I am Ifren Cuevas. This is the second year I'm coming to Canada and the truth is it is good to work in this country for through it I am pulling my family forward. But what I don't like are the Indian bosses because they discriminate against us and also they give us bad housing to live in and they like to see us as lower than themselves. In this country we are worth the same, regardless of which country you come from.   State of Veracruz

16. Ramón Holguin, Camago, Chihuahua

Ramon Holguin Soy de Camago Chihuahua y megustaria que nos otoren la Residencia al tiempo de las temporus y nos respeten y seamos todos yguales y mas benefisios para todos y mejorar los salarios porque aqui la vida es muy cara y no rinde bien y uno deja todo en Mexico   grasias

Ramon Holguin I am from Camago, Chihuahua and I would like that they allow residency after a time and they respect us and we are all equal and more benefits for all and to improve the salaries because here life is very expensive and it doesn't stretch and one leaves everything in Mexico. Thank you.

14

17. Israel Dominguez, Tabasco

Mi nombre es Israel Dominguez Vengo de Tabasco. Y me gustaria que el govierno Canadiense me facilitara traer a mi familia a Canadá. Tambien me gustaria que hubiera un intercambio de ver las costumbres que los Canadienses visiten Tabasco. Tambien que los digan a los patrones Hindu que no vean a los trabajadores Méxicanos
Como esclavos sino que los valoren. Gracias.

My name is Israel Dominguez. I am from Tabasco. And I would like that the Canadian government will help me bring my family to Canada. Also I would like that there be an exchange to see our customs, that the Canadians visit Tabasco. Also that they tell the Hindu bosses not to see the Mexican workers like slaves, but that they value them. Thank you.

18. Cruz, Tabasco

Mi nombre es Cruz y soy del Estado de Tabasco. Mi proposito de estar aqui en Canadá un pais bonito pero quisiera que el gobierno canadiense se interesara en superbisar q los patrones de la India que son muy duros con nosotros los trabajadores ya que nosotros nos entrejamos con todo el trabajo. Adios.

My name is Cruz and I am from the state of Tabasco. My purpose/intention to be here in Canada, a pretty country, but I would like that the Canadian government will be interested in supervising the bosses from India who are very hard with us workers, because we are committed to do all the work. Good bye.

19. Alejandro M. V.

Mi nombre es Alejandro M. V. Estoy muy orgulloso de estar con ustedes aqui en Canadá gracias a este programa. Mi familia tiene casa, comida, escuela. Me siento muy orgulloso de mi familia de mis hijos pero me siento en estos 6 meses muy triste al no estar con ellos pero lo se que pronto pasara el tiempo para estar con eyos y quisiero estar todo el tiempo con ellos pero ya se que no es possible. Gracias.

My name is Alejandro M. V. I am very proud to be here with you in Canada thanks to this program. My family has a house, food, school. I feel very proud of my family, of my children but I feel in these 6 months very sad to not be with them, but I know that the time will pass quickly to be with them and I want to be with them all the time, but I already know that is not possible. Thank you.

20. Carlos V., Tuxtepec, Oaxaca

Soy Carlos V. estado: Tuxtepec, Oaxaca. Me deseo es que primeramente busquen a Dio que las cosas vienen por añadidura. Dios les bendiga umilde trabajado de Jesuchristo.

I am Carlos V. state: Tuxtepec, Oaxaca. My wish is that first they seek God, that things come in addition. God blesses the humble worker of Jesus Christ.

21. J. Isabel Arellano, Hidalgo

Me llamo J. Isabel Arellano Soy del Estado de Hidalgo. Yo no mas quiero que boloren nuestro trabajo y que me los miren y nos tartan como objetos de trabajo y que algun dia podemos traer nuestra familia. Grasias.

I am J. Isabel Arellano. I am from the state of Hidalgo. I just want that our work be valued and that they look at us and they treat us like work objects, and that someday we can bring our family. Thank you.

22. Rodolfo, Puebla

Mi nombre Rodolfo Puebla   a mi me gusta Canadá Todo esta bien pero solo hay una cosa que no me gusta es de que nos demos trabajos muy pesados y el Los Patrone siempre te exijen cada ve mas en especial los patrones Indianos a pesar de que tenemos un bajo sueldo y malas viviendas y retrosos en los pagos de quiensena y nunca supervisan ni nos dan equipos de trabajo.

My name is Rodolfo. Puebla. I like Canada. Everything is good but there is just one thing that I don't like it is that they give us very heavy work and the boss always demands every time more, especially the Indian (Indo-Canadian) bosses in spite of the fact that we have low pay and bad living conditions and they are behind in the bi-monthly payments and never supervise nor give us work equipment

23. Pedro M. G.

Pedro M. G. Me gustarian mas grantias como trabajador porque no todos ce hucan valer. Tambien me gusturia poder arreglar mis papeles para poder traer a mi familia tenienco un meior sueldo no estoy de acuerdo en el trato de los patrones Indianos.

Pedro M. G. I would like more guarantees as a worker because not everyone asserts worth. Also I would like to be able to organize my papers to be able to bring my family, to have a better pay, and I don't agree with the treatment of the Indian (Indo-Canadian) bosses.

24. Martín

Me yamo Martin Me gusta travajar en Canadá y me gustaria traer a mi familia aunqe fuera de vacaciones y viajar por Canadá mas que nada conoser lugares como todos sus lagos ermosos.

I'm Martin. I like to work in Canada and I would like to bring my family even if for vacations and to travel across Canada to know more places, like all its beautiful lakes.

18

25. Lazaro Alvarranto

Lazaro Alvarranto, Mexicano deseo que el pays de Canadá nos de la oportunidad de traer a mi familia y deseo que dios bendiga muchisimos el pays de Canadá

Lazaro Alvarranto, Mexican. I wish that the country of Canada give us the opportunity to bring my family and I wish that God blesses greatly the country of Canada.

26. Armando, Quintana Roo

Soy Armando y vengo a Canadá para poder darles una major vida a mi familia y me gustaria que nos dieran visa para poder traer a nuestras familias.

I am Armando and I come to Canada to be able to give a better life to my family and I would like that they give us visas to be able to bring our families.

27. Raymundo

Pues me gustaria mucho si Dios permite ser como los Canadienses y poder traer mi familia por los menos para los vacaciones para conocer Canadá junto con ellos y que traten bien nuestros patrones porque hay companeros de trabajo que no les admistlen? en su lugar de vivienda calefaccion lavadora y aqua caliente.

Well I would like it a lot if God merits that I be like the Canadians, and to be able to bring my family, at least for vacations to know Canada together with them and that our bosses treat us well because there are coworkers who don't have heat, a washing machine and hot water in their housing.

28. Abdias Tecalco Barojas, Veracruz

Mi nombre es Abdias Tecalco Barojas del Estado de Veracruz. Me duele el alma dejar mi familia en México cada que vego a Canadá, pero tengo que trabajar para ellos. Ojala un dia pudieran venir conmigo, es mi deseo.... Dios Primero. Asi sera.

My name is Abdias Tecalco Barojas from the state of Veracruz. My soul hurts to leave my family in Mexico every time I come to Canada, but I have to work for them. Hopefully one day they will be able to come with me, it is my wish. God First. So it will be.

Me yamo
Jesus ALFREDO
Me gusta venir
a canada por que el trabajo
es Bueno y asi Le doy un
Mejor sustento a mi Fami
y La sake adelante Tanvie
me gustaria que Dieran
visa Para Poder traerla
aki. Yo vengo de
ciudad constitucion
B.C.S
y Tengo
2 años viniendo

JOSE Tomás
Robles Ealindo
Es la segunda bes que
bengo.
soy de S.n Adres Buenavis
ta Tlaxcala.
Estoy aca Para el
vienestar de mi
Familia

Me llamo
Atilano Balam
Tengo 6 temporada aca
en canada me gustaria
que su beran el salerio y que
el gouverno entre que visas
Para nuestra familios
soy de Cancun quintanaRoo

soy ANTONIO
Bengo de Mexico
y vivo en Tlaxcala
llevo 8 años viniendo
a CANADA Para darles mejor
vida a mi familia y a mis
Padres y Kisiera
Traerlos Para que
conoscan

29. *Jesús Alfredo, Baja California Sur*

Me yama Jesus Alfredo Me gusta venir a Canadá por que el trabajo es bueno y asi le doy un major sustento a mi familia y la sake adelante Tamvien me gustaria que dieran visa para poder traerla aki Yo vengo de Ciudad Constitucion, B.C.S. y tengo 2 años viniendo.

I'm Jesus Alfredo. I like to come to Canada because the work is good and in this way I give a better support to my family and pull them forward. Also I would like that they give a visa to be able to bring them here. I come from Ciudad Constitucion, Baja California Sur and I have been coming for two years.

30. *José Tomás Robles Galindo, San Andres Buenavista, Tlaxcala*

Jose Tomás Robles Galindo Es la segunda bes que bengo. Soy de Sn. Andres Buenavista, Tlaxcala. Estoy aca para el vienestar de mi familia.

Jose Tomás Robles Galindo. It is the second time that I come. I am from San Andres Buenavista Tlaxcala. I am here for the well being of my family.

31. *Atilano Balam, Quintana Roo*

Me llamo Atilano Balam Tengo 6 temporada aca en Canadá Me gustaria que subieran el salario y que el govierno entregue visas para nuestra familias Soy de Cancun, Quintana Roo.

I'm Atilano Balam. I have 6 seasons here in Canada. I would like that they raise the salary and that the government deliver visas for our families. I am from Cancun, Quintana Roo.

32. *Antonio, Tlaxcala*

Soy Antonio Bengo de Mexico y vivo en Tlaxcala Llevo 8 años viniendo a Canadá para darles major vida a mi familia y a mis padres y kisiera (quisiera) traerlos para que conoscan.

I am Antonio. I come from Mexico and live in Tlaxcala. I have been coming for 8 years to Canada to give a better life to my family and my parents and I would like to bring them so they can know about (Canada).

SOY IZHAR
JIMENEZ MORALES
Y SOY d CHETUMAL QUINTA
ROO Yevo 2 temporadas
Viniendo A canadá y vengo
X mejorar mi casa y
darle una cochera A
MIS HIJOS y MUCHAS
GRACIAS X d gOBNOS
TSAWWAR

ABElardo del Rio Llamas
de villanu y me siento contento conesta
oportunidad de trabajo que me dieron
en canadá por que Gracias A elle e sa
bido salir Adelante con mis Hijos
de escuela y en General como Gr
A ello también y ce mi casa por que n
tenia y ci me gustaria la oportuni
dad de las Visas para la familia
Para que conocieran canadá

MEllAMO
JAVIER soy de Hidalgo
lleve años trabalando aqui
en canadá y la sente es muy
amable con todos nosotros
y Lo que quisiera es que el
gobierno permita que nuestros
familiares nos visiten que
no les Pongan muchas trabas
Para que sea fácil la entrada
A canadá.

HOLA MY NOMBRE
ES CIRILO SOY
DEL ESTADO DE MEXICO
ES MY 1° BES EN OLIVER
Y AQUI LA JENTE SE VE QUE
I SON MUY BUENAS PERSO
NAS QUICIERA QUE NO NOS
BIERAN COMO BICHOS RAROS
SALUDOS AL MINISTRO
DE CANADA
ATTA CIRILO

33. Izhar Morales, Chetumal, Quintana Roo

Soy Izhar Jimenez Morales y soy d Chetumal Quinta Roo yevo 2 tenporadas viniendo a Canadá y vengo x (que) megorar mi casa y darle una carrera a mis hijos y muchas gracias que d jarnos trabajar.

I am Izhar Jimenez Morales and I am from Chetumal, Quintana Roo. I have two seasons coming to Canada and I come to improve my house and give a career to my children; and thank you very much to allow us to work.

34. Abelardo Del Rio Llamas

Ola me lamo Abelardo del Rio Llama y me siento contento con esta oportunidad de trabajo que medieron en Canadá proque gracias a ello he podido salir adelante conmis hios de escuela y en general como a elle tambien y en mi casa porque noş(?)tenia y ci me gustaria la oportunidad de las visas para la familia para que conocieran Canadá

Hi. I'm Abelardo del Rio Llama and I feel content with this opportunity of work that Canada gives me because thanks to Canada I can advance with my children in school and in general (like Canada/elle too) and in my house because we have it and yes, I would like the opportunity of visas for the family so that they can know Canada.

35. Tahir, Hidalgo

Me llamo Tahir Soy de Hidalgo Llevo 9 años trabajando aqui en Canadá y la gente es muy amable con todos nosotros y lo que quisiera es que el govierno permita que nuestros familiars nos viciten que no les pongan muchas trabas para autorisarle la entrada a Canadá.

I'm Tahir. I am from Hidalgo. I've been working here in Canada 9 years and people are very friendly with all of us and what I would like is that the government permits our families to visit by not making difficult the permit entrance to Canada.

36. Cirilo de la Rosa, Estado de México

Hola my nombre es Cirilo Soy del Estado de Mexico Es me 1o (primer) bes en Oliver y aqui la gente se ve que son muy buenas personas Quiciera que no nos bieran como bichos raros. Saludos al Minstro de Canadá. Attn Cirilo

Hi. My name is Cirilo. I am from the state of Mexico. It is my first time in Oliver and here the people seem to be very good people. I would like that they don't see us as "strange insects" (weirdos). Greetings to the Minister of Canada. Attentively, Cirilo.

37. Salvador Sandoval, Querétaro

Mi nombre es Salvador Sandoval. Soy de Queretaro. Me gustaria que algun dia nos dieran papeles.

My name is Salvador Sandoval. I'm from Queretaro. I would like that someday they would give us papers.

38. Felix Ortega Delgado, Durango

Felix Ortega Delgado. Santiago Papasquiaro, Durango. Me gustaria poder traer mi familia que tanto estraño

Felix Ortega Delgado Santiago Papasquiaro, Durango. I would like to be able to bring my family that I miss so much.

39. Mariano Demeza, Chiapas

Mi nombre es Mariano Demeza Soy del Estado de Chiapas Es mi primer año en venir en Canada y haber y ojala que todo valla bien en el trabajo y la salud.

My name is Mariano Demeza. I'm from the state of Chiapas. It's my first year to come in Canada and let's see and hopefully that everything goes well in work and health.

40. Baltazar Lopez Ruis, Veracruz

Baltazar Lopez Ruis Que a todos nos baya vien Veracruz, México.

Baltazar Lopez Ruis That everything goes well for all of us. Veracruz, México.

Crossing Over: The Art of Deborah Koenker

By Liz Wylie

Art should have political, spiritual, and surprising elements. It should try to find new language of communicating in order to give awareness to the public. Then every society can use the layer it needs at the moment. If one is interested in the political, they can take that. If the next one needs spiritual, it can be found in the same work. So if you just did one level, for example only political, it's like an old newspaper, you read it today and tomorrow it's old news. The art dies. Art with this kind of complexity has many lives where many societies can take something different at different times. It can live for centuries, otherwise who cares?

— Marina Abramovic

The sort of complexity or multi-valence that artist Marina Abramovic speaks of as necessary for an engaged art to have lasting power is in fact one of the hallmarks of success in the work of Vancouver-based artist Deborah Koenker. Koenker does not produce art that is simply placards for causes – her projects always function deeply as art – with strong visual impact, deep emotional and psychological aspects, and satisfyingly complicated layers of meaning. There is a process of transformation that occurs in Koenker's hands, as she takes the issues she is concerned about and sets out to give them visual expression in her work. US Poet Laureate Juan Felipe Herrera (who has a text in this publication) has said that when you turn something into art, you honour it. This hard-won achievement has been the kernel at the heart of Koenker's practice since she began working as an artist.

Building on her previous bodies of work, Koenker became interested several years ago in producing a project about the Mexican agricultural workers in the Okanagan. These men and women come here under Canada's Seasonal Agricultural Workers Program (SAWP), and provide low-cost work in greenhouses, farms, vineyards, and orchards for up to eight months (per person) of any given year. Koenker arranged to make visits to this region over a three-year period, travelling up and down the Okanagan Valley, meeting with workers, their support workers, and with owners of vineyards and orchards. She was struck by how much the workers missed their families and their own cuisine and culture, and she was impressed by the enormous personal sacrifices the workers make to come here in order to earn money to support their loved ones.

She began work on the *Grapes and Tortillas* exhibition without a preconceived idea about the completed installation. It grew from her interest in the situation of the Mexican workers here and took shape organically over time. She herself had gained a large Mexican family by marriage in 1976, and has visited that country many times. Several of her previous bodies of work have been initiated in response to conditions there, beginning with her lyrical and fanciful *The Mexican Night* suite of thirteen prints from 1981-3.

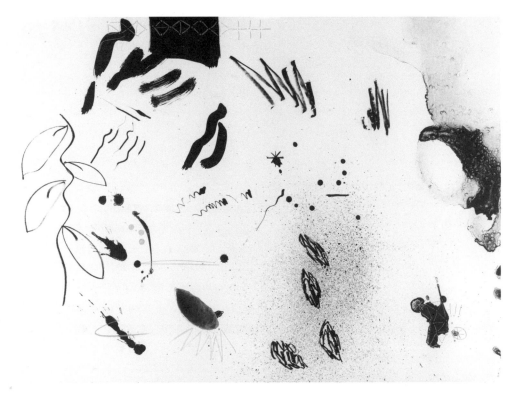

Deborah Koenker, *Tango: The Mexican Night*, 1981, colour lithograph on BFK Rives, 22 ½ x 30 in. (57 x 76 cm).

Deborah Koenker, *San Miguel: The Mexican Night*, 1982, colour lithograph on BFK Rives, 22 ½ x 30 in. (57 x 76 cm).

The title for this project was taken from that of a 1970 book of travel ruminations and poems by American Beat poet Lawrence Ferlinghetti about his time in Mexico in the 1960s. The relaxed and heady atmosphere Ferlinghetti and Koenker both evoked is from a time now past, tragically, as Mexico is no longer the peaceful paradise it once was, both for its citizens and visitors. Much of this change is due to the North American Free Trade Agreement that came into effect in 1994, the details and consequences of which will be discussed in detail in other texts in this publication. The negative changes have been profound.

During her visits to the Okanagan Koenker began to take photographs of the Mexican workers she met here, thinking at first she would pair images of single faces with photograph of fruits. The idea was to acknowledge the role the workers had in supplying these fruits to our markets. Later she had the inspired idea of having each participant hold up a flour tortilla (a staple of the Mexican diet) as a blank slate on which s/he wrote his or her name with black marker, adding where they were from, and a thought or comment about working in Canada, or what they missed from home. The intense impact of each of these people both naming themselves and giving voice to their personal experiences strengthens the overall effect of the photographs, and the large number of Koenker's portraits (there are 160 in the exhibition) adds a further freight to the feeling a viewer has from looking at them *en masse*. The power of language is something Koenker has explored in her work quite often. In her case, this has nothing to do with words in and of themselves – the derivations of words, for example – but for the ideas words can convey, and the emotions they can invoke. Thus, she successfully complicates her "straight" photographic portraits by adding the personal contribution of each sitter, to powerful effect.

In the twenty-first century we are surrounded by works of art that have social or political content, but in fact, this is a fairly recent phenomenon in the history of Western art. In earlier eras, artists who strove to have their art openly embody a social conscience were few and far between. This was largely due to the patronage situation for artists up until the mid-nineteenth century or so, when art for art's sake began and the artist was freed up to starve in his or her garret. Previously it would not have gone well for an artist advocating for the underdog when being paid by an aristocrat or the church. There was Goya, as a notable exception, of course, particularly with his *Disasters of War* etchings and *The Third of May* (1808), an oil painting depicting the martyrdom of Spanish freedom fighters at the hands of one of Napoleon's firing squads.

Francisco Goya, *The Third of May 1808*, 1814, oil on canvas. Collection of the Prado Museum, Madrid.

Edouard Manet, generally associated with the French Impressionists, quoted from this work of Goya's when creating his own group of paintings about the Execution of Maximilian in Mexico (the event was in 1867, and Manet's works were completed during the next two years).

Edouard Manet, *The Execution of Emperor Maximilian,* 1867-9, oil on canvas. Collection of the Kunsthalle Mannheim, Mannheim, Germany.

Contemporary with him (just a little older) and also in Paris was Honoré Daumier, a brilliant satirist and caricaturist of men in the legal profession and politicians.

Honoré Daumier, plate from *Les Gens de Justice,* 1840s, lithograph.

With the dawn of the twentieth century and the spread of the avant garde in art, artists with social consciences began bearing witness to injustices in their own times and circumstances. The German artist Kathe Kollwitz (1867-1945) paved the way with her anti-war work followed the German Dada artists in raking politicians and the upper classes over the coals.

Kathe Kollwitz, *Seeds for Planting Should not be Ground,* 1942, lithograph.

The Russian avant garde harnessed their collective talents to the wheel of utopian socialism, and in Mexico and the USA in the 1930s, socialist realism was born, which would be the approach approved for art in the Maoist era in China, especially in the Cultural Revolution of the 1970s. *Guernica,* painted by Picasso in 1937, the most famous "protest" work of art in the first half of the twentieth century, depicted the bombing of women and children in a Basque village by German and Italian forces during World War II.

Depression-era photographers such as Walker Evans and Dorothea Lange produced strong images that conveyed the economic devastation of the time as it affected masses of disenfranchised Americans, most particularly of the Dust Bowl exodus.

Dorothea Lange, *Migrant Mother*, 1936, photograph.

Later, in the 1960s, photo-journalism created and disseminated hard-hitting images that galvanized millions of people around issues such as the Vietnam War and black civil rights in the US.

Modern and contemporary artists around the world have moved aggressively into the political and social realms. Whereas modernist art of the 1960s and 70s and Minimalist art from the same time were both self-referential, artists of the post-modern age became free to embrace any kind of social concerns in their practices. In fact, these days art that does *not* make reference to the social is now sometimes shunned and given negative monikers in the art press, such as zombie formalism and crapstraction.

All of this looking back is intended to provide an art historical and contemporary art context for the practice of Deborah Koenker, moving

as she has in her unfolding career, from earthy abstract sculptural installations and meditative, investigative work in printmaking, into exploring photography, installation (at times with audio components), and embroidery (with its links and references to women and women's labour) that is intense and emotional with its social content. With her exploration of photography that is part portrait, part social document, Koenker is furthering the tradition of revolutionary photographers such as Robert Frank, who changed how we conceived of a photographic portrait.

Trained in the 1970s in drawing, printmaking, and sculpture, Koenker arrived in Vancouver to live in 1973, not knowing anyone. Within a short time she became one of the founding members of the Malaspina Printmakers Workshop, which opened in 1975, and where she remained active as workshop director for many years. She went back to art school in 1985 for an MFA in sculpture/installation (at Claremont Graduate University in Claremont, California). By this time, feminism had come to the fore in academia and the art world, and Koenker embraced the issues involved.

It seems that printmaking, with its democratic notion of the multiple, and its basis so often in communities of artists, can sometimes form a fertile springboard for artists to move into other forms of artistic expression. Koenker gradually stopped producing prints for the most part, and also sculptures *per se*, as discrete objects, and became increasingly interested in installation. The beautiful and arresting six-foot-diameter piece made from driftwood titled *Rootball* in her *Bar-Ba-Loot* show at the OR Gallery in Vancouver in 1992 was the last example of her former aesthetic-object-based practice.

Deborah Koenker, *Rootball*, from the artist's *Barbaloot* installation 1992, driftwood.

In the late 1990s Koenker made two series of prints, *Path of a Body* (1996-7), and *Punctuation* (1999-2002). These were gentle works, with the small bits of texts in *Path of a Body* encouraging the viewer to "rest when tired," for example. The specific meaning of the punctuation work is elusive, although the images of old-fashioned floral fabrics juxtaposed with semi colons, colons, parentheses and the like, were straightforward images to read visually. Perhaps these prints were linked to the notion of pausing, as punctuation is often about setting up rests between words and phrases, and the soothing floral fabrics are almost soporific.

Deborah Koenker, *You are the sky*, *Path of a Body* series, 1996-7, transfer print, 8½ x 12 in. (20.9 x 30.4 cm)

Deborah Koenker, *Adrift*, 1999, installation view at the Richmond Art Gallery.

Deborah Koenker, *Vingette, Puncuation* series, 1999, transfer print, 6 x 10½ in. (16.2 x 26.9 cm)

In 1999 the artist produced a full-scale installation for her solo show *Adrift*, at Open Space in Victoria, BC, and at the Richmond Art Gallery, Richmond, BC. In this piece the viewers meandered their way between curved walls made of white paper, illuminated from behind. A strip of black linear images at eye level ran along the undulating paper walls. The theme for this was chronic but invisible illness, transformed into the metaphor of a physical journey for the gallery-goer.

She had learned various embroidery stitches when a child, and turned to these abilities in a piece she began in 2002, that is still unfinished and ongoing. Titled *Learning to Draw*, it is comprised of small squares of white silk onto which the artist transferred details from drawings and engravings by various Old Masters. She has then been embroidering over these with this traditionally female medium, called needlework in the nineteenth century. The components are highly beautiful and Koenker subtly makes her point about the fate of so much of women's labour as artists as having disappeared, while the more highly valued male artists' work in drawing and painting was preserved in museums. Koenker has

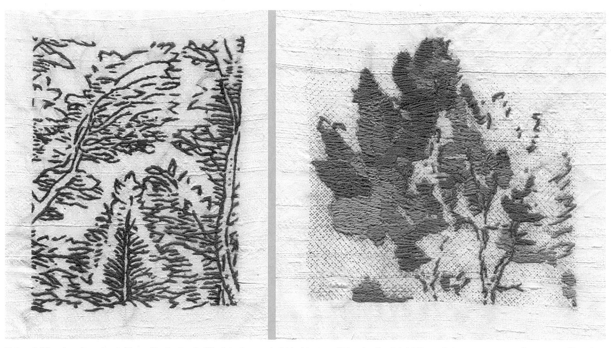

Deborah Koenker, *Learning to Draw: illustration for The Satyric scene in L'Architettura (Sebastian Sergio)*, 2002, work in progress, transfer print and hand embroidery on duppioni silk, 5½ x 4½ in. (13.9 x 11.4 cm); Deborah Koenker, *Learning to Draw: Landscape with a man killed by a snake, #1 (Nicolas Poussin)*, 2002, work in progress, transfer print and hand embroidery on duppioni silk, 4¼ x 4¼ in. (10.7 x 10.7 cm).

Deborah Koenker, *Learning to Draw: engraving after Titian drawing from Encyclopedie by Diderot and d'Alembert, #1*, 2002, work in progress, transfer print and hand embroidery on duppioni silk, 4⅝ x 6¼ in. (11.4 x 15.8 cm).

Deborah Koenker, *Learning to Draw: Landscape Sketch #1 (Jean-Honoré Fragonard)*, 2002, work in progress, transfer print and hand embroidery on duppioni silk, 5¼ x 6½ in. (13.3 x 16.5 cm).

continued to explore sewing and embroidering with textiles in her practice. With socially oriented work in contemporary art often the materials become part of the message (to paraphrase Marshall McLuhan). We might consider the Chinese dissident artist Ai Weiwei, for instance, and his use of wooden stools or real life-vests cast off on the beaches in Turkey by Syrian migrants, and other unusual art materials in his pieces, which call attention to and comment on current issues from around the world.

Koenker's overall journey as an artist has involved a kind of crossing over, referred to in the title of this essay – a crossing over from traditional to non-traditional, even political media, and from primarily formalist or aesthetic concerns to social ones, although she has continued to embrace the beautiful.

In 2003, building on her work in installation, and her knowledge of the Spanish language and connections in Mexico, the artist began work on a Mexican-based project that would take three years to complete, and would involve eighty-four volunteer participants. Titled *Las Desaparecidas* (in English, The Missing Ones), the work stemmed from the horrific situation of the many women murdered in Ciudad Juárez in Mexico. By now the news coverage of these murders has made the situation common knowledge internationally. (It was perhaps described in most dispassionate yet gruesome and emotionally disturbing detail in the massive work of fiction called *2666*, by the late Chilean-born writer Roberto Bolaño, published posthumously in 2004.) Koenker felt compelled to deal with these murders head on in an art project. She was able to meet with a group of people in Tapalpa, in Jalisco, Mexico, and worked

Deborah Koenker, *Las Desaparecidas,* 2007, installed at the Templo de San Antonio Centre Cultural, Tapalpa, Jalisco, Mexico.

to win their trust, so that they agreed to use the images of their own fingerprints as embroidery patterns. They then met to stitch as a group, hand embroidering onto long bands of unbleached cotton over greatly enlarged transfer prints of their own fingerprints as patterns. The embroideries were installed at the Galeria Manuel Felguerez, at the Universidad Autonoma Metropolitana in Mexico City in 2006 in a solo show. (The work was subsequently shown in four other venues: the Kathrin Cawein Gallery, Pacific University, Forest Grove, Oregon in 2007; the Guggenheim Gallery, Chapman University, Orange, California in 2007; the Templo de San Antonio Centre Cultural, Tapalpa, Jalisco, Mexico in 2007; and the Richmond Art Gallery, Richmond, BC in 2008.)

Perhaps the most redolent of these several installations of *Las Desaparecidas* was the one in the deconsecrated church in Tapalpa, Jalisco, in which the draped and suspended lengths of fabric alluded to liturgical vestments and altar cloths. The large scale of the work is extremely important as it gives the work gravitas and commands attention the way fingerprints at their actual size would not. Fingerprints themselves are loaded notions. On the one hand, they identify each one of us as ourselves alone. But they are used by police everywhere in databases of criminals and of missing persons. So they become fraught images, and our minds provide the more negative associations as we contemplate the work.

With her accomplishment of winning the trust of the people in Tapalpa to work with her on *Las Desaparecidas*, Koenker created a work that opened up a new direction for her practice that she has continued to explore. As well, she has been fortunate to travel to residencies such as the Canada Council's Paris Studio in 2011, and in 2015 to artists' residencies in Cadiz and Barcelona in Spain. She continues to take photographs, especially when travelling, and often creates fairly large-scale, thematic montages using her digital images.

With her current installation, *Grapes and Tortillas*, at the Kelowna Art Gallery, Deborah Koenker set out to provide gallery-goers with an intense taste of life in Mexico, with its colour and vibrancy, the people's joy in food and family, and their religious devotion. At the same time, she wanted to include references to the darker issues surrounding, for example, the crossing of the American border. So the exhibition includes a seventy-one-foot-long mural of colour photographs Koenker made in 2008 of the border fence/wall between Mexico and the US. These images form a stark contrast to the photographic portraits included on other walls. In conjunction with the fence/wall mural, Koenker has included on the wall some excerpts from a

Deborah Koenker, ribbons at the Bascilica of Our Lady of Guadalupe Shrine, Mexico City, 2012.

Deborah Koenker, vineyard netting, Naramata, 2015.

poem (published in a book with the same title that includes other texts and materials) by Juan Felipe Herrera called *187 REASONS MEXICANOS CAN'T CROSS THE BORDER*. There is a bittersweet quality to this poem with its biting humour overlaid onto a tragic social situation.

Bisecting the entire gallery space and hanging in a vertical plane from the ceiling is a giant curtain made from vineyard netting that has been interwoven with 2000 lengths of colourful ribbons (one for each of the temporary workers placed here in the Okanagan each year), making reference to a common devotional ritual at shrines in Mexico. This piece forms an enormous soft sculpture, somewhat in the vein of Koenker's *Las Desaparecidas*. It both dominates and divides the space and sets the tone for the overall installation. Koenker has titled the piece *La Frontera* (The Border), as it is also a metaphor for the cultural and language barrier the Mexican workers face while they are here.

In one alcove to the left of the gallery's entrance Koenker has set up various materials and photographic murals that make reference to a typical Mexican kitchen. Domestic spaces like this are the warm centres of a home, and where conversations go on, as well as cooking. The notion of food continually touched on throughout the exhibition is a loaded one, as the Mexican crops and their cycle of renewal is under threat by GMO seeds. Koenker intends this kitchen facsimile as a tribute to a woman known as Doña Vicky, an activist from Oaxaca who was a leader in stopping a McDonald's restaurant from opening in 2002 in the historic town square of her city. Koenker has included references to food in the exhibition as it is a hot issue in Mexico, where their ancient cycle of planting and harvesting is under threat by GMO seeds that have suicide genes, preventing them from being reproduced in subsequent seasons.

Across the gallery space, on the other side of the net, a sort of quasi-shrine has been set up, with wooden chairs facing a large image of the Virgin of Guadalupe, the patron saint of Mexico. On each chair the artist has placed a votive candle and a printed enlarged reproduction of a Loteria card. Real Marigold blossoms, which will be refreshed throughout the duration of the exhibition, will be set out on the shrine. A selection of old Okanagan wooden orchard ladders has been assembled in this area as well.

Koenker also created a playlist for the exhibition, comprised of music that one might hear while visiting Mexico, which plays over the sound system of the gallery space. These include tracks by Lhasa de Sela and Lila Downs. In a darkened area she is looping some of her own images, projected as stills.

The artist's achievement with this installation has not been an easy one: to convey the culture of another place to gallery visitors here, and to do so with accuracy, respect, and sensitivity. Her main goal with this aspect of the exhibition was to show audiences the richness of the culture in Mexico that the temporary workers miss when they are here, away from their families. Koenker hopes that viewers come away with an enhanced awareness of the real, true cost of food, and who is paying the price for it.

Koenker has the unerring ability as an artist to transform base materials into vehicles of thought and emotion. She bypasses our internal gatekeeper and penetrates deeply into our consciousness with her art. Within the trajectory of her own artistic career, she has made a shift from a materials-based practice to one of social commentary and activism. With the notion of crossing over comes the idea of connection, and this is another of Koenker's skills – connecting with the people who are the basis of her research and the subjects for her work, and connecting with the gallery goer. This can be traced back in her practice to 1987 with an elevated wooden walkway she built with her husband, architect Roberto Pacheco, for viewing the cherry tree in her back garden. This structure also connected the adjoining back gardens of the neighbours, and not just physically, but at a deep human level – aesthetically and spiritually. This would seem to still be the goal in Koenker's art and it is one that she so successfully achieves.

Deborah Koenker and Roberto Pacheco, *The Cherry Tree Project*, 1987, three adjacent Vancouver gardens.

Liz Wylie has been curator of the Kelowna Art Gallery since 2007. As well as her work as a curator, she has been writing reviews and articles on contemporary and historical Canadian art since 1977. Her recent publications include monographs on the Canadian artists Keith Langergraber, John Hartman, Bill Rodgers, Christos Dikeakos, John Hall, and Landon Mackenzie. Wylie holds an MFA in art history from Concordia University in Montreal.

41. Rubín Medina, Colima

Mi nombre es Rubín Medina Soy del Estado de Colima, México. Esta bien venir a trabajar aca para sacar el sustento de la familia seguiremos aqui hasta que se acaba la corrupción de nuestro pais asta entonces estamos aca.

My name is Rubín Medina. I'm from the state of Colima, México. It is good to come to work here to draw the livelihood of the family. We will continue here until the corruption of our country is finished. Until then we will be here.

42. Felipe de Jesús Mera, Hidalgo

Mi nombre Felipe de Jesus Mera y soy del Estado de Hidalgo. Primero quiero agradeser al gobierno de aqui por el trabajo que nos dan y espero ellos tambien les guste nuestro trabajo.

My name Felipe de Jesus Mera and I am from the state of Hidalgo. First I want to thank the government here for the work they give us and I hope they also like our work.

43. José Abele Bucio Saucedo, Los Reyes, Michoacán

Jose Abele Bucio Saucedo   Los Reyes Michoacan quiero ver mi familia.

Jose Abele Bucio Saucedo   Los Reyes Michoacan. I want to see my family.

44. Aniceforo Valladaros Bustos, Guerrero

Mi nombre es Aniceforo Valladaros Bustos Estado Guerrero. Me gusta este pais porque no hay violencia. Quiero que enseñen para aprender en diferentes trabajos. Muchas Gracias.

My name is Aniceforo Valladaros Bustos, state of Guerrero. I like this country because there isn't violence. I want that they teach us to learn different kinds of work. Thanks very much.

MI NOBRE
CRISTOBAL PEREZ
REYES. YO. SOY.
ESTADOS Oaxaca.
ME GUSTA ESTAR.
CANADA

LiZANDRO DZib EK
Calkini Campeche
Quiero que Mi Familia
siempre esten UNiDOS
y se sienton Orgullosos
de Mi trabajo y
Agradesco mucho
A CaNada por
La Oportunidad
de poder estar
aqui

Me llamo
Eladio Mejia Maturano
y
Dengo del Estado de Hidalgo
y mi deseo es
Consuelo Para toda mi familia
en especial a mi Padre y tia
Ha hora que mi abuelito
esta muy grabe y enmermo
Para mi que estoy lejos

Ciprianos Azpeitia Cano
SO Salvado Oaxaca
que Hgo
H esta bien jida mi
Familia y H mis sueños
Se agan Realidad
Gracias

45. Cristobal Perez Reyes, Oaxaca

Mi nombre Cristobal Perez Reyes. Yo soy Estados Oaxaca. Me gusta estar Canada.

My name is Cristobal Perez Reyes. I'm from the state of Oaxaca. I like to be in Canada.

46. Lizandro Ozib EK, Calkini, Campeche

Lizandro Ozib EK   Calkini, Campeche. Quiero que mi familia siempre esten unidos y se sientan orgullosos de mi trabajo y agradesco mucho a Canada por la oportunidad de poder estar aqui.

Lizandro Ozib EK   Calkini, Campeche. I wish that my family may always be united and they feel proud of my work and I thank Canada a lot for the opportunity to be able to be here.

47. Eladio Mejia Maturano, Hidalgo

Me llamo Eladio Mejia Maturano y bengo del Estado de Hidalgo y mi deseo es Consuelo para toda mi familia en especial a mi padre y tios Ha hora que mi abuelito esta muy grabe y cansado(?) para mi que estoy lejos.

I am Eladio Mejia Maturano and I come from the state of Hidalgo and my wish is comfort for my whole family, especially for my father and uncles now that my grandpa is very sick and I am far away.

48. Cipriano Azpeitia Cano, San Salvador Actopán, Hidalgo

Cipriano Azpeitia Cano San Salvador Actopan Hgo K esten bien toda mi familia y k mis sueños se agon realidad. Gracias.

Cipriano Azpeitia Cano San Salvador Actopan, Hidalgo. That my whole family may be well and that my dreams become reality. Thank you.

49. Martín, Michoacán

Martin Michoacan

Martin Michoacan

50. Emilio Isidro Reyes, Tepic, Nayarit

Emilio Isidro Reyes   Tepic Nayarit   Desea que a todos los migrante nos ayude dios.

Emilio Isidro Reyes   Tepic Nayarit   I wish that God helps all us migrants.

51. Miguel Peralta G., Nayarit

Miguel Peralta G de Nayarit   que lo pasen bien.

Miguel Peralta G from Nayarit. That everyone has a good time.

52. Raul Miguel Diaz Arroyo, Mexicali Baja California Norte

Raul Miguel Diaz Arroyo   Mexicali B.C. Norte   Ke en el mundo no sufran los niños.

Raul Miguel Diaz Arroyo – Mexicali B.C. Norte That the world's children don't suffer.

53. *Fermin Mota Nuñez---Tepic, Nayarit*

Fermin Mota Nuñez Tepic Nayarit México Bienestar Salud y quiero tener a mi familia con migo si pudiera traerla para estar siempre unidos como siempre lo emos estado. Gracias por ellos.

Fermin Mota Nuñez Tepic, Nayarit, Mexico Well being, health and I want to bring my family with me if I could bring them along to be always together as we have always been. Thanks on their behalf.

54. *Jesús Bautista*

Jesus Bautista me gustaria trabajar sin preocupaciones y poder traer mi familia aqui. Me deseo es tener un major sueldo y major oportunidades de trabajo.

Jesus Bautista I would like to work without concerns and to be able to bring my family here. My wish is to have better pay and better work opportunities.

55. *Jaime Lopontzi, Aztatla San Jose, Tlaxcala*

La Malintzi (montaña) Soy Jaime Lopontzi vengo Aztatla San Jose Tlaxcala México

La Malintzi (mountain) Jaime Lopontzi – I am Jaime Lopontzi I come from Aztatla San Jose Tlaxcala México

56. *Aurelio Bautista H., Toctitlán Tlanchinor, Hidalgo*

Me llamo Aurelio Bautista H. y bengo de la comunidad de Toctitlan Tlanchinor "Hidalgo" México

My name is Aurelio Bautista H. and I come from the community of Toctitlan, Tlanchinor "Hidalgo", Mexico

TULA De Ayende
Jose Luis Perez Monroy
Je creo que me baya bien
i todo Cen Borito

Nivardo Ramos
Oaxaca Mexico, trabajando
Estoy Aqui trabajando
duro Para Mejorar
Economico para
Mi Familia

Ambar Uriel
En cañada Trabajando,
soy D Armeri colima

Extrañando
A mi
Familia
LOS AMO

Soy MARTHA Ruiz
bengo de Campeche Camp
Me gusta estar en canada
Trabajando me gusta todo lo unico
que Follaria para estar permamente
es tener un poco mas de tiempo
para trabajar en canada

57. José Luis Perez Monroy, Tula de Allende

Tula de Allende   José Luis Perez Monroy deceo que me baya bien I todo cea bonito.

Tula de Allende   José Luis Perez Monroy I wish that everything goes well with me and everything will be good.

58. Nivardo Ramos, Oaxaca

Nivardo Ramos   Oaxaca México Estoy aqui trabajando duro para mejorar economia para mi familia

Nivardo Ramos—Oaxaca Mexico   I'm here working hard to improve the economy for my family.

59. Ambar Uriel, Armería, Colima

Ambar Uriel En Canada trabajando Soy d Armevi Colima Extrañando a mi familia. Los amo.

Ambar Uriel   In Canada working. I'm from Armeria, Colima. Missing my family. I love them.

60. Martha Ruiz, Campeche

Soy Martha Ruiz Bengo de Campeche Comp Me gusta estar en Canada trabajando me gusta todo lo unico que faltaran para estar plenamente es tener un poco mas de tienpo para trabajar en Canada.

I am Martha Ruiz I come from Campeche, state of Campeche. I like to be in Canada working. I like everything. The only thing I miss to be complete is to have a little more time for work in Canada.

61. *Bertha Fellipa Haas UC, Campeche*

Mi nombre es: Bertha Fellipa Haas UC. y soy de Pomuch Campeche y bengo atrvajar para mis hijos y espero en dios que me baya muy bien aca mi pensamiento es de que los Canadiense nos traten bien y que por nesesidad vengo. Gracias dio les vendiga.

My name is: Bertha Fellipa Haas UC. and I am from Pomuch, Campeche and I come to work for my children and I trust in God that things go very well with me here. My thought is that the Canadians treat us well and that for necessity I come. Thank you. God bless you.

63. *Aurora Cruz Carcamo, Misantla, Veracruz*

Aurora Cruz Carcamo Vengo de Misantla Veracruz Tengo tres hijos Estoy contenta por poder venir a Canada a trabajar. Gracias te doy dios por aberme dado esa oportunidad de conoser canada

Aurora Cruz Carcamo I come from Misantla Veracruz. I have three children. I am content to be able to come to Canada to work. I give God thanks for having given me this opportunity to know Canada.

62. *Leticia Bustamante Frias, Estado de México*

Leticia Bustamante Frias Vengo del Edo. de Méx Me gusto el haber venido a Canada pero si me gustaria que siempre tuviera la oportunidad de venir por mas de 2 meses ya que yo tengo mi hijo y lo tengo que dejar solo y muchas veces se le dejo a mi mamá pero lo hace de mala gana y eso me hace sufrir mucho mas sin encambio si me dieran mas tiempo hay una posibilidad de que mas pronto deje de viajar y asi poder estar más tiempo con mi hijo y de esa manera seria ser totalmente feliz.

Leticia Bustamante Frias I come from the state of México. I like to have come to Canada but I would like that I still would have the opportunity to come for more than 2 months since I have my son and I have to leave him alone and many times I leave him with my mother but she does this with bad spirit and this makes me suffer a lot more; in the event that they would give me more work there is a possibility that I could stop traveling sooner and that way be able to be more time with my son and in this way I would be totally happy.

64. *Virginia Montalvo Angeles, Tlaxcala*

Hola. Mi nombre es Virginia Montalvo Angeles Soy del Estado de Tlaxcala. Estoy orgullosa porque gracias a esté programa y al esfuerso de mi trabajo e superado un poco el nivel economico di mi familia. Tengo dos hijos los cuales e sacado adelante , y primero Dios le segire pidiendo me siga dando fuerza y salud para seguir adelante. Muchas Gracias.

Hi. My name is Virginia Montalvo Angeles I'm from the state of Tlaxcala. I am proud because thanks to this program and the effort of my work I have improved a little the economic level of my family. I have two children who I have raised, and first I ask God to keep following me and to keep giving me strength and health to continue forward. Many thanks.

Leticia Suarez
Yo bengo del D.F. y estoy muy
Agradecida con los canadienses
Por darnos la oportunidad de
trabajar en este país porque
Gracias a estoy saliendo adelante
con mi familia y tambien Gracias
A Dios por permitirme llegar
asta Aca

HOLA!!! Mi nombre es
es bely Ramon Mtz.
Le doy gracias a Dios x haberme
Permitido estar en este maravilloso lugar yo vengo de San Luis P.
te doy gracias a canada x haberle
permitido a los mexicanos entrar
a este su país y brindernos la
oportunidad de conocernos y salir
adelantegracias canada que Dios
te bendiga para que siga
ayudando a Mexico y porque
seamos uno solo.

Tomas Silva Romero
Ola Soy De Durango
y meda mucho gusto
como ser mucha Jente
K Lo alluda en este Payz
Con el idiona y Cone estan
comportores mexicanos

SOY LARA
Olivia
VALENZUELA VENGO
DE MEXICO DEL ESTADO DE
SINALOA CIUDAD CULIACAN TENGO
DIAS TRABAJANDO AQUI EN CANADA,
ESTOS AQUI TRABAJANDO PARA PODER
MANTENER A MIS 4 HIJOS EN MEXICO
BOI PADRE Y MADRE PARA ELLOS
DESEO DE CORAZON SEGUIR VIVIENDO
PARA OBTENER ESTABILIDAD ECONOMICA
CA J PODER SOLVENTAR Y AYUDAR A
MIS HIJOS GRACIAS DOY A ESTE
PAIS POR DARME LA OPORTUNIDAD
DE TRABAJAR Y AYUDARME
♡ MEXICO ←→ ♡ CANADA

52

65. Leticia Suarez, Distrito Federal

Leticia Suarez Yo bengo del D.F. y estoy muy agradecida con los canadienses por dar nos la oportunidad de trabajar en este pais por que gracias a esto e salido adelante con mi familia y tambien gracias a dios para permitirme llegar asta acá.

Leticia Suarez I come from D. F. and I am very grateful with the Canadians for giving us the opportunity to work in this country because thanks to this I have gone forward with my family and also thanks to God for permitting me to arrive here.

66. Bely Ramón Martinez, San Luis Potosi

Hola!!! Mi nombre es Bely Ramón Martinez. Le doy gracias a Dios x habereme permitido estar en este maravilloso lugar. Yo vengo de San Luis P. Le doy gracias a canada x haberle permitido a los mexicanos entrar a su pais y brinder nos la oportunidad de conocernos. y salir gracias canada que Dios bendiga para que sigas ayudando a México y porque seamos uno solo.

Hi!!! My name is Bely Ramón Martinez. I give thanks to God that has permitted me to be in this marvelous place. I come from San Luis Potosi. I give thanks to Canada that has permitted the Mexicans to enter their country and give us the opportunity to meet. And to leave. Thank you Canada. That God bless you for continuing to help Mexico and because we are one.

67. Tomá Silvo Ramero, Durango

Tomá Silvo Ramero Ola soy de Durango y meda mucho gusto como ser mucha jente que lo alluda en este payz en el idioma y como estan conpaneros mexicanos

Tomá Silvo Ramero Hi I am from Durango and it pleases me how many people in this country help with the language and how they are fellow Mexicans.

68. Olivia Lara Valenzuela, Estado de México

Olivia Lara Valenzuela Vengo de México del Estado de Sinoloa ciudad Culiacan Tengo dias trabajando aqui en Canada. Estoy aqui trabajando para poder matener a mis 4 hijos en Mexico Soy padre y madre para ellos. Deceo de Corazon seguir viviendo para obtener estabilidad economica y poder solventar y ayudar a mis hijos Gracias doy a este pais por darme la oportunidad de trabajar y ayudarme. (corazon) Mexico (corazon) Canada

Olivia Lara Valenzuela I come from Mexico, the state of Sinoloa, the city Culiacan. I have days working here in Canada. I am here working to be able to support my 4 children in Mexico. I am father and mother for them. I wish with my heart to continue living to obtain economic stability and to be able to solve and help my children. I give thanks to this country for giving me the opportunity to work and help myself. (heart) Mexico (heart) Canada

69. *Alejandra Rodriguez, Aguacalientes, Aguacalientes*

Hola soy Alejandra Rodriguez de Aguacalientes Solo espero que este trabajo en Cánada valga la pena el sacrificio de dejar a nuestra familia tan lejos y muchas Gracias por las personas que nos asen sentir vien y los que no tambien. GRACIAS

Hi I am Alejandra Rodriguez from Aguacalientes I only hope that this work in Canada is worth the sacrifice of leaving our family so far away and many thanks for the people who make us feel well and also those who don't. THANKS.

70. *Flor Leiticia Rodriguez Lopez, Monterrey, Nuevo León*

Monterrey Nuevo Leon   Flor Leiticia Rodriguez Lopez Vengo a Canada para sacar adalante a mis hijos vk soy madre soltera y k con lo k gana en Canada puedo vivir major para tdo mi Fam: y poder salir a delante a mis hijos k son 3 varones y con mucho gusto vengo aka y espero k algun dia vayan a Mty. N. L. para k los conoscan y vayan a comer conjunto(?) Mil gracias x pedirme para trabajar Gobierno k bajan los impuestos.

Monterrey Nuevo Leon   Flor Leiticia Rodriguez Lopez I come to Canada to pull my children up because I am a single mother and with what I earn in Canada I can give a better living to my whole family. And to be able to raise my children that are 3 boys and with much pleasure I come here and hope that some day you come to Monterrey Nuevo Leon so that you can know it and come to eat together. A thousand thanks that you ask me to work. That the government lower the taxes.

71. *Abelina, Aguascalientes, Aguascalientes*

Hola Mi nombre es Abelina para pedir al gobieno canadiense que baje los impuestos Soy de Aguascalientes. Grasias

Hi My name is Abelina To ask the Canadian government to lower the taxes. I am from Aguascalientes. Thanks.

72. *Rosalba Gonzaléz Marquéz, Veracruz*

Hola Soy Rosalba Gonzaléz Marquéz de Veracruz Espero que este sacrificio devenir tan lejo valga las Pena. Dejar a todo mi sere querido.

Hi I am Rosalba Gonzaléz Marquéz from Veracruz. I hope that this sacrifice to come so far is worthwhile. To leave all my dear ones.

73. *Aurora Perez Roldán*

de México para Canada   Hola. Soi Aurora Perez
Roldán   Me gusta muxo Canada   Gracias por avenos
permitido entrar a este pais I darnos la oportunidad de
estar con estas personas canadienses. Esperamos no de
fraudarlos y que algun dia nos pueden ver como nos
merecemos. Lla que todos somos hermanos que dios iso
iquales tal ves diferente lenguaje pero los dos somos
iquales todos necemos a un solo Dios   Mis deceo es
que cuando necesitamo ayudarnos unos a los otros.

From Mexico to Canada. Hi, I'm Aurora Perez
Roldán. I like Canada a lot. Thank you for having
permitted to enter this country and give us the
opportunity to be with these Canadian people.
We hope not to let you down and that some
day you could see us as we deserve. Because
we are all brothers that God made equal, maybe
different language but both are all equal, born by
a single God. My wish is that when I need help
we help each other.

74. *Faviola Medina, Oaxaca*

Faviola Medina   Asta la Victoria siempre   Oaxaca

Faviola Medina Until victory always. Oaxaca

75. *Irma Gutierrez Peña, Limones Cosautlán,*
Veracruz

Irma Gutierrez Peña Vive la vida al maximo
porque no sabes cuando dejaras de hacerlo. Limones
Cosautlán Veracruz

Irma Gutierrez Peña Live life to the maximum
because you don't know when you'll stop living.
Limones Cosautlán, Veracruz

76. *Marceil Zuñiga, Querétaro*

Hola Mi nombre es Marceil Zuñiga Soy del estado
de Queretaro estoy orgullosa por mis logros en el
programa y le doy gracias a dios y espero lograr algo
mas para darles una major vida a mi familia.

Hi My name is Marceil Zuñiga. I'm from the
state of Queretaro. I am proud for my earnings in
the program and I give thanks to God and hope
to earn something more to give a better life to my
family.

77. Yasuri Pool Mayorga, Quintana Roo

Hola mi nombre es Yasuri Pool Mayorga soy del Estado de Quintana Roo Estoy orgullosa de estar en el programa de estar en el xq con este puedo sacar adelante a mis hijos y a mi mamá le doy gracias x ayudarme le doy las Gracias y los quiero mucho Gracias

Hi my name is Yasuri Pool Mayorga. I am from the state of Quintana Roo. I am proud to be in the program to be in it because with it I am able to pull forward my children and I give thanks to my mamá for helping me. I give them thanks and I love them a lot. Thank you.

78. José Maria Cheverria, Colima

José Maria Cheverria   Pues antes q nada Un Saludo a todos los lectures Cuento con seis temporada biniendo. Muchos grasias por la oportunidad de contar con este empleo. Grasias a los gobiernos por las oportunidades q nos brindan. Grasias

José Maria Cheverria   Well before anything a greeting to everyone. I count 6 seasons coming. Many thanks for the opportunity to count on this employment. Thanks to the governments for the opportunities that it provides us.

79. Antonio Meraz A, La Ciudad, Durango

Antonio Meraz A — Durango Dgo

Antonio Meraz A — Durango Durango

80. Victor M Portillo Garcia, Guerrero

Victor M Portillo Garcia — Gerrero Mexico

Victor M Portillo Garcia — Gerrero, Mexico

Seeing the Unseen:
160 Views of a Foreign Worker

By John Vaillant

I live in Canada.
Temporarily.
I work a lot.

— Lorenzo Tome

A century ago, a graveyard opened in the mind of the lawyer and poet, Edgar Lee Masters, and from it emerged the late inhabitants of a small American town. One by one, the freed spirits of Spoon River rose up and spoke, adding epilogues to their epitaphs, their wish: to be witnessed by the living, to be seen for who they truly were. In this way, over the course of some two hundred poems, the men and women in Masters' "Spoon River Anthology" reveal their carefully guarded secrets and dreams.

It has been years since I read "Spoon River Anthology," but it was the memory of those voices that echoed in my head when I first encountered the host of people represented in Deborah Koenker's show, each with a message, a wish to be witnessed. *Grapes and Tortillas* is a multi-media installation, but at its heart are 160 photographed portraits. At half life-size, it feels almost like their subjects are right there in the room. Almost, but not quite. As close as they may seem, their messages, written with a Sharpie on large tortillas, come to us from a remove as distant as turn-of-the-century Spoon River. These people, too, are temporary visitors from another world.

My soul hurts to leave my family in
  Mexico,
but I have to work for them.
God willing, one day they will be able to
  come with me.
It is my wish.

— Abdias Tecalo Barojas

The Mexican guest workers depicted in *Grapes and Tortillas* are here by the fickle grace of the Mexican and Canadian governments. They come from a world so remote that some first-timers step off the plane having no idea where they've landed beyond the country of Canada, an abstract notion at best. Once through customs, they are taken straight to the farm, orchard or vineyard where they will spend the next two to six months. Whether it's in Quebec or British Columbia doesn't really matter; there won't be much time for sightseeing. Isolated by language, long workdays and limited transportation, these men and women exist in a kind of economic internment - near us, but not of us, with few opportunities for contact or exploration.

I thank Canada a lot
for the opportunity to be here.

— Lizandro Ozib EK

We hope not to let you down and
that someday
you could see us as we deserve.

           – Aurora Perez Roldán

When most of us think of the Okanagan Valley or, more generally, of the people who make British Columbia's fruit, vegetables and wine possible, Mexicans don't leap to mind. Even if you were to take a drive into that hot, dry, surprisingly fertile country, the fact that Mexican laborers were working the fields you saw beyond your windshield might never occur to you. It's even less likely that you would guess their numbers. The subjects of Koenker's show represent only a fraction of the total number of Mexicans currently participating in Canada's forty-year old Seasonal Agricultural Worker Program (SAWP). In 2016, roughly 6,000 temporary workers – more than the entire population of Osoyoos – will be working in the fields and warehouses of southern B.C. These numbers are up threefold over the past decade, and are expected to grow nationwide.[1] [Of this number, about 90% are Mexican nationals with the remaining 10% coming from Jamaica and, more recently, Guatemala.] For this reason, the scores of faces looking back at us with their frank, what-you-see-is-what-you-get expressions, raise some uncomfortable questions about work, about Canada, about the value of food, and about the rights of the people who feed us.

I would like to be treated with equality
and the rights of dignity due a human
   being,
not to be seen only as a worker
   to be exploited.

           – Aureo Guerrero Sanchez

Once, while on a train in the Russian Far East, I wandered into a carriage filled with North Korean "guest workers" bound for remote logging camps. The moment I stepped through the door, I was almost immobilized by their otherness: they looked so different from everyone else on the train, and even if they had been willing to make eye contact, there was no way to communicate with them. It was clear they were forbidden to leave their compartments. I was struck both by the yawning gulf between us, and by how little autonomy they had - unthinkable (I assumed then) in a First World country.

I want Canadians not to look at us as
   oddballs,
because we are all equal.

           – Julian

As beneficial as Mexican workers are to the Canadian farmers who employ them and to those of us who consume – literally – the fruit of their labours, and as grateful as these workers are for a wage many times greater than what they could earn at home, the imbalance in liberty and status is inescapable. Though not as extreme, their situation resembles that of the North Korean loggers: while in Canada, they are tethered to their respective farms and, at the end of the season, they too will be sent home. While many similarities can also be found between our "guest workers" and the Chinese and Indian laborers who did so much of the heavy lifting during British Columbia's formative years, there is one crucial difference: the Indians and Chinese were allowed to stay.

We hope that someday [Canadians] take
   note
that we are good workers and,even more,
as people who are pulling forward
with the heavy and tiring work of this
   country.

           – Manuel Domínguez

Most of the money these seasonal workers earn – $10.49 an hour, minus food, housing, and all applicable taxes – is sent home to support families in a country where the minimum wage is roughly $5.00 a day[2],and 20% of the population does not even eat regularly. In Mexico, these Canadian remittances are truly a boon, paying for food, housing, education and down payments on plots of land. Because these workers' status here is so precarious, doing anything that might disrupt this crucial flow of money, such as complaining about unsafe or unsanitary conditions, or trying to unionize, can be risky. Even if you're not fired outright, you might not be invited back the following season. So, there is an implicit message to keep your head down and your mouth shut, a lesson the North Koreans on that Russian train learned early and well.

> What I don't like are the [Indo-Canadian] bosses
> because they discriminate against us, and also they give us bad housing to live in.
> And they like to see us as lower than themselves.
> – [name withheld to protect the identity of participant]

The Okanagan Valley appears beautiful and accommodating, but it is not a simple place; cultures from three continents have been colliding there for more than a century, and foreign seasonal workers add another layer of complexity to the mix. But this is Canada, and negotiating these differences - for good and ill - has been at the core of the national project for the past 400 years. It is not an overstatement to say that this – mediating and accommodating broad diversity – is a defining characteristic of a "true Canadian." This is the real gift of Koenker's show: the opportunity to bridge that cultural gulf and meet some of the people who are doing jobs that most Canadians have become too wealthy and comfortable to consider doing themselves. "It's not such a big leap," says Koenker, "to have some empathy when you think that your grandparents did the same thing a couple of generations ago."

The 160 labourers who appear to be gazing out at us from the walls of this gallery are also gazing into Canada from a parallel world, somewhere between North Korea and Spoon River. And we, gazing back, may discover that we are looking into a mirror. Even if we can't see ourselves, we may see our ancestors, those other foreign workers who gaze back at us now from other photographs on other walls.

Endnotes
1. Christine Mittler - RAMA
2. https://www.littler.com/publication-press/publication/mexico-approves-increase-daily-minimum-wage-2016

John Vaillant is a freelance writer whose work has appeared in *The New Yorker, The Atlantic, National Geographic,* and *The Walrus.* His first book, *The Golden Spruce* (Knopf, 2005), was a bestseller and won several awards, including the Governor General's Award for Non-Fiction. His second nonfiction book, *The Tiger* (Knopf, 2010), is also an award-winning bestseller. His latest book, a novel, is *The Jaguar's Children* (Knopf, 2015).

81. José Luis Avolos, Guanajuato

José Luis Avolos Soy de Guanajuato Mi deseo que todos mis paisanos mexicanos regresemos con bien a mexico para estar nuevamente con nuestras familias

José Luis Avolos I'm from Guanajuato My wish that all my fellow Mexican countrymen go back well to Mexico to be with our families anew.

82. Israel Honostroza D., San Rafael de Abajo, Coahuila

Hola Me llamo Israel Honostroza D. Soy del estado de Coahuila Mi pueblo se llama San Rafael de Abajo Estoy muy orgulloso de estar laborando en Canada para poder sacar a mi familia adelante CANADA MEXICO

Hi My name is Israel Honostroza D. I'm from the state of Coahuila. My town is called Lower San Rafael. I am very proud to be labouring in Canada to be able to pull my family forward. CANADA MEXICO

83. Gaspar Ayala Cardona, San Marcos Mpio de San Pedro, Coahuila

Mi nombre es Gaspar Ayala Cardona Soy de ejido San Marcos Mpio de San Pedro Coahuila y me siento orgulloso de trabajar en Canada para el bienestar de mi familia.

My name is Gaspar Ayala Cardona. I am from the community San Marcos of San Pedro, Coahuila and I feel proud to work in Canada for the well being of my family.

84. Apolonio Bastidas, Sinaloa

Hola Soy Apolonio Bastidas soy de Sinaloa Pues estoy muy contento de venir a trabajar a Canada Saludos para todos Canada Sinoloa

Hi I'm Apolonio Bastidas. I'm from Sinaloa. Well I am very content to come to work in Canada. Greeting to everybody. Canada Sinoloa

85. *José Luis, Distrito Federal, México*

Hola Soy José Luis y soy DF Topilejo y estoy muy contento diber benido a Canada a trabajar saludos a todos

Hi I'm José Luis and I'm from D. F. Topilejo and I'm very contented to have come to Canada to work. Greetings to everybody.

86. *Javier Hernández, Distrito Federal, México*

Javier Hernández Distrito Federal México (Hecho de menos)
-Familia
-Comida. Mole, carnitas
-Fiestas

Javier Hernández Distrito Federal México (I miss)
-Family
-Food. Mole, carnitas
-Parties

87. *Angel Dominguez, Estado de México*
Angel Dominguez Edo. México (Hecho de menos)

-Familia
-Comida (carnitas, mole)
-Pachangas

Angel Dominguez Edo. México (I miss)
-Family
-Food. (carnitas, mole)
-Parties

88. *Jorge A. Herrera*

Jorge A. Herrera (Hecho de menos)
-Comida
-Familia
-su gente
-la misa los domingos

Jorge A. Herrera (I miss)
-Food
-Family
-one's people
-mass on Sundays

89. Jesús Salazar, Tonalá, Chiapas

Jesús Salazar   Tonala, Chiapas
Extrañando a la familia, la comida y el deporte

Jesús Salazar   Tonala, Chiapas
Missing the family, the food and sports.

90. Pedro Alonzo Flores, Santa Cruz Atizapán, Estado de México

Pedro Alonzo Flores   Estado de México, Santa Cruz Atizapan
Lo que estaño de México
1. la comida
2. la familia
3. y las mujeres

Pedro Alonzo Flores   Estado de México, Santa Cruz Atizapan
What I miss of Mexico is
1. the food
2. the family
3. and the women

91. Aldo Vazquez Lopez, Coaxitlán, Morelos

Aldo Vazquez Lopez   Coaxitlan Morelos
Extraño a mi hijos esposa padres comida

Aldo Vazquez Lopez   Coaxitlan Morelos
I miss my children, wife, parents and the food.

92. Agustin Morales V., San Gregorio, Michoacán

Agustin Morales V. San Gregorio   Mich
Regresar bien
estrallo a México
10 en Canada

Agustin Morales V. San Gregorio   Michoacan
(I wish) to return well (to Mexico).
I miss Mexico
10 (years) in Canada

TABASCO MEXICO
ME GOSTA MI TRABAJO
CANADA ES SEGURO
MEXICO NO

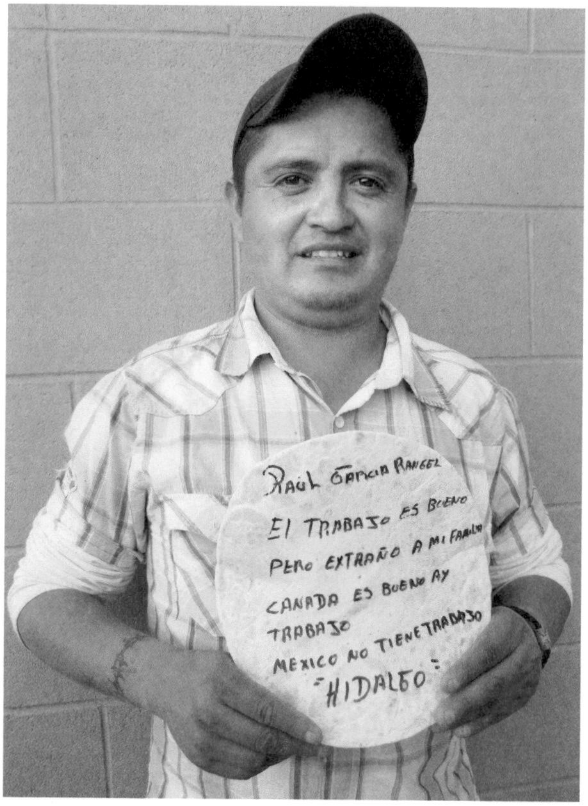
Raúl García Rangel
El TRABAJO ES BUENO
PERO EXTRAÑO A MI FAMILIA
CANADA ES BUENO AY
TRABAJO
MEXICO NO TIENE TRABAJO
"HIDALGO"

Jorge Reyes
estado de puebla
Extraño
el
Pozole
mole poblano
Las quesadillas
y
extraño mucho.
a mi familia

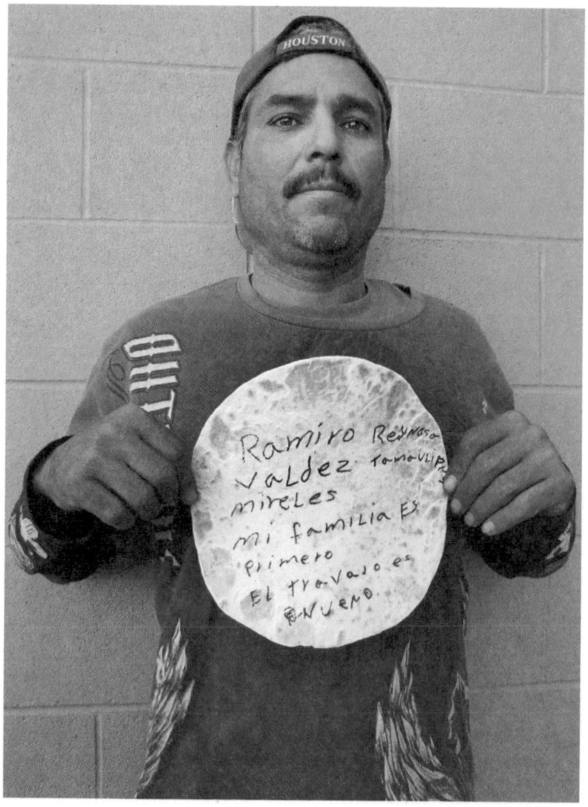
Ramiro Reynosa
Valdez Tamaulipas
mireles
mi familia ES
primero
El travajo es
Bueno.

93. *Ignacio Garcia Meudel, Tabasco, México*
Ignacio Garcia Meudel   Tabasco, México
Me gusta mi trabajo. Canada es suguro. México no.

Ignacio Garcia Meudel   Tabasco, México
I like my work. Canada is secure. Mexico no.

94. *Raul Garcia Rangel, Hidalgo*

Raul Garcia Rangel
El trabajo es bueno pero extraño a mi familia
Canada es bueno ay trabajo
México no tiene trabajo
"Hidalgo"

Raul Garcia Rangel
The work is good but I miss my family
Canada is good, there is work.
Mexico doesn't have work.
"Hidalgo"

95. *Jorge Trujido Reyes, Puebla*

Jorge Trujido Reyes — Estado de Puebla
Estraño el pozole, mole poblano, quesadillas y estraño
mucho a mi familia.

Jorge Trujido Reyes — State of Puebla
I miss pozole, mole poblano, quesadillas and I
miss my family a lot.

96. *Ramiro Reynasa Valdez, Tamaulipas*

Ramiro Reynasa Valdez   Tamaulipas
Mireles mi familia es primero
El trabajo es bueno

Ramiro Reynasa Valdez   Tamaulipas
Look, my family is first.
The work is good.

97. Uvaldo Olivera Juarez, Yucatán

*Uvaldo Olivera Juarez Vengo del estado de Yucatan.
A mi megustaria que emberdad tubieramos los mismos
derechos que cual kier persona que viva en Canada.
Que fueramos tratado de igual manera. y que valoren
el sacrificio que hacen uno para venir tan lejos para
sacar adelante a nuestras familias.*

Uvaldo Olivera Juarez I come from the state of
Yucatan.
I would like that we would really have the same
rights as any person in Canada. That we would
be treated in the same way.
And that they would value the sacrifice that
one makes to come so far to pull our families
forward.

98. Fausto Moreno Pochoteco, Guerrero

*Mi pueblo Ayahualco
Me yamo Fausto Moreno Pochoteco Soy de Gerero.
Me gustaria que el gobierno me diera la oportunida de
trae a mi familia a canada A mi me usta aqui en
canada a mi me gustaria bibir*

My town is Ayahualco. My name is Fausto
Moreno Pochoteco.
I would like that the government give me the
opportunity to bring my family to Canada. I like
it here in Canada I'd like to live here.

99. José Becerril Alcantara, Estado de México

*6 de Agosto del 2015
Soy José Becerril Alcantara. Tengo 50 años. Soy del
Edo. de México Municipio de Jilotecpec. Espero este
vien. Le doy mis mas cinseras gracias por darme la
oportunidad de trabajar en Canada quiciera me dieran
la oportunidad de q un miembro de mi familia me
visitara algun dia para q se diera cuenta como es el
trabajo de aca. Gracias Canada y Govierno.*

6 August 2015
I am José Becerril Alcantara. I am 50 years old.
I'm from the state of Mexico, city of Jilotecpec.
I hope you be well. I give my most sincere
thanks for the opportunity to work in Canada
and I would like to have the opportunity that a
family member could visit me someday to take
account of the work here. Thanks Canada and the
government.

100. Luis F. T. G., Jalisco, México

*Luis F. T. G. Jalisco, Mx 2015 08 06
Al principio Canada era un sueño inalcancable. Ahora
lo es mi familia.*

Luis F. T. G. Jalisco, Mexico 2015 08 06
In the beginning Canada was an unreachable
dream. Now it is my family.

74

101. *Eustorgio Ceron Ruiz, Altzayaca, Tlaxcala.*

Gracias Dios Mio por darme la oportunidad de aportar a la economia personal al programa de imigrantes mexico canada a este pais tan hermoso q' es Canada y a mi Familia por apoyarme, a mi esposa y a mis 4 hijas: Aby, Silvia, Yeny, Mary, Nico. Soy Eustorgio Ceron Ruiz de Altzayaca, Tlaxcala.

Thanks to my God for giving me the opportunity for the personal economic support of the immigrant program between Mexico-Canada in this country so beautiful that is Canada and my family for supporting me, and my wife and my four daughters: Aby, Silvia, Yeny, Mary, Nico. I am Eustorgio Ceron Ruiz de Alzayaca, Tlaxcala.

102. *Rogelio Narciso Ocampo, Ixtapa, Guerrero*

6- Agosto 2015
En la comunidad de Coswton B.C. Mi Buena y mala esperiencia es porque estoy lejos de mi familia y despues la felicidade por que tengo mucho trabajo en este pais. Tengo todo lo que necesito. Soy feliz. Soy de Ixtapa, Guerrero. Rogelio Narciso Ocampo.

6 August 2015

In the community of Cawston B.C. My good and bad experience is because I am far from my family and then happiness because I have a lot of work in this country. I have everything I need. I am happy. I am from Ixtapa, Guerrero. Rogelio Narciso Ocampo.

103. *Ignacio, Puebla*

¡Hola! Soy Ignacio. Soy originario de Puebla. Llevo 9 años en el programa de trabajadores agricolas. Y la verdad me da mucho gusto trabajar aqui. Y honestamente entre mas tiempo paso pienso si habra valido la pena haber dejado toda una vida aqui en Canada.
Seria maravillosa saver que valio la pena y que algun dia se nos pudiara otorgar alguna oportunidad de residir aqui en Canada. Doy gracias por este espacio. Que nos brindan gracias.

Hi! I'm Ignacio. I'm originally from Puebla. I have 9 years in the program of agricultural workers. And the truth is that I like the work here a lot. And honestly as more time passes I wonder if it is worthwhile to spend a whole life here in Canada.
It would be wonderful to know that it was worthwhile and to some day have the opportunity to reside here in Canada. Thank you for this space. Thank you

104. *Miguel, Hidalgo*

HOLA Soy Miguel del estado de Hidalgo. Tengo 6 años trabajando en CANADA. En un pueblo lleno de gente hermosa y caritativa.
Uno de mis grandes sueños es tener mi Familia aqui en este gran pais que me adado mucho. Me gustaria quel govierno Canadiencse algun dia nos de esa grandiosa oportunidad. Gracias

HI I'm Miguel from the state of Hidalgo. I have 6 years working in CANADA. In a place full of beautiful and caring people.
One of my greatest dreams is to have my Family here in this great country that has given me much. I would like that the Canadian government someday gives us this great opportunity. Thank you.

105. Ariel Cruz Rosas, Michoacán

Hola: Mi nombre es Ariel Cruz Rosas y soy de Michoacan México. Soy un trabajador agrícola aqui en Canada y le agradezco al gobierno de Canada por darme la oportunidad de entrar a trabajar, y quisiera que nos diera una recidencia permanente y aprovecho para enviarle un cordial saludo y muchas gracias.

Hi: My name is Ariel Cruz Rosas and I'm from Michoacan Mexico. I'm an agricultural worker here in Canada and I thank the government of Canada for giving me the opportunity to come to work, and I'd like that they would give us permanent residency and I take this chance to send a cordial greeting and many thanks.

106. Aureo Guerrero Sanchez, Hidalgo

Hola. Soy Aureo Guerrero Sanchez vengo de Hidalgo, Mexico, me gustaria que nos trataran con igualidad con los dignos derechos que debe tener un ser humano que no nos miren solamente como trabajadores a los que pueden esplotar. Me gustaria que nos permitieran entrar a este paiz con visa por tiempo indefinido y traer a nuestras familias. Gracias Canada.

Hi. I am Aureo Guerrero Sanchez I come from Hidalgo, Mexico, I would like to be treated with equality and the rights of dignity due to a human being, not to be seen only as a worker to be exploited. I would like that we could come to this country with a permanent visa and to bring our families. Thank you Canada

107. Miguel Vásquez Rubio

Miguel Vásquez Rubio. Grasias a Dios que puedo estar en Canada. Pero tambien quiesiera que mis hijos estudiaran aqui en Canada y traer toda la familia porque es duro dejar La Familia.

Miguel Vásquez Rubio. Thanks to God that I am able to be in Canada. But also I'd like that my children study here in Canada and to bring my whole family because it is hard to leave the Family.

108. Jose Sabino Flores Barranco, Chignauhapan, Puebla

Soy de Chignauhapan Puebla Mexico. Tengo 8 años trabajando en Oliver. Me gustaria que algun dia mi familia pudiera venir a saludarme de vacaciones como visita de turista. Grasias esto deseo. Jose Sabino Flores Barranco.

I'm from Chignauhapan, Puebla, Mexico. I have 8 years working in Oliver. I would like that someday my family would be able to come to see me on vacation on a tourist visa. Thank you for this wish. Jose Sabino Flores Barranco.

109. Victo Quisehuatt, Puebla

Victo Quisehuatt de estado de Puebla. Tengo 15 años trabajando en Canada y Canada es un pais marabiyoso y gracias a este pais emos salido adelante por darnos trabajo grasias nostra sacrifisio tambien. Canada a tenido mucho de los mexicanos.

Victo Quisehuatt, state of Puebla. I have 15 years working in Canada and Canada is a marvelous country and thanks to this country we have gone forward through hard work, thanks to our sacrifice also. Canada has had a lot from Mexicans.

110. Genaro Garibaldi Astorga, Sinaloa

Genaro Garibaldi Astorga Soy de Sinaloa Gracias a CANADA por la oportunidad de trabajo. Tengo 3 años viniendo me gustaria que me dieron la oportunidad de que me vicitara mi "Familia"

Genaro Garibaldi Astorga I'm from Sinaloa. Thanks to CANADA for the opportunity of work. I have 3 years coming , I like that they give me the opportunity to bring my "Family."

111. Juan Ramón, Oaxaca

Llevo 3 años trabagando en canada me gustaria que alguen dia mi familia me visitara Soy de Oaxaca orgullosamente.

I have 3 years working in Canada. I'd like that someday my family could visit me. I'm proudly from Oaxaca.

112. Abel Vazquez, Hidalgo
Abel Vazquez
Soy de Hidalgo Mx.
Mi primer año me paresio una experiencia muy agradable. Me gustaria que el gobierno nos permitiera que la familia pueda visitarnos , tener mas beneficios y un sueldo mejor. Saludos a todos los paisanos.

Abel Vazquez
I'm from Hidalgo Mexico.
My first year was a very agreeable experience. I would like that the government allows that the family visit us, to have more benefits and better wages. Greetings to all my countrymen.

Manuel de Jesús Mancilla Cruz
7 Años de
Trabajo en Canada
Chiapas — Mexico
Cintalapa Chiapas

Agradesco a Dios por estar en
Canada y siempre mantenerme para
Hacer mi trabajo lo mejor
que se puede.

Gonzalo Guzmans
Banderas del Aguila
Durango Dgo
Me gustoria
que vinieron mi
Familia

LEOBARD
SANCHEZ GARCIA
10 AÑOS DE TRA-
BAJO BUINA ESPE
RIENSA DE CONBI
BIA CON CANADIE
NEES X MEXICANO
HUAXTLALA

CORNELIO FLORES A.
AMECAMECA EDO. MEXICO

TRABAJO EN KELOWNA Y ME
GUSTA LO QUE HAGO EN CANADA

CUISIERA QUE TODOS LOS MEXICA-
NOS QUE VENIMOS A CANADA DEMOS
EL ESFUERZO SIEMPRE PARA
TRABAJAR

*113. Manuel de Jesús Mancilla Cruz, Cintalapa,
Chiapas*

*Manuel de Jesús Mancilla Cruz   7 años de trabajo en
Canada.*
Chiapas—Mexico
Cintalapa Chiapas
*Agradesco a Dios por benir a Canada y siempre
mantenerme bien hacer mi trabajo lo mejor que se
pueda.*

Manuel de Jesús Mancilla Cruz   7 years working
in Canada.
Chiapas—Mexico
Cintalapa Chiapas

I thank God for coming to Canada and always
keeping me well to work as best as I'm able.

*114. Gonzalo Guzmans, Banderas del Aguila,
Durango*

*Gonzalo Guzmans   Banderas del Aguila, Durango,
Dgo*
Me gustaria que viniera mi familia

Gonzalo Guzmans   Banderios del Aguila,
Durango, Durango
I would like that my family could come.

115. Leobard Sanchez Garcia, Itaxtlala

*Leobard Sanchez Garcia   10 años de trabajo buina
esperiensa de conbibir con canadiences y mexicanos.
Itaxtlala.*

Leobard Sanchez Garcia   10 years of work, good
experience to live with Canadians and Mexicans.
Itaxtlala.

*116. Cornelio Flores A., Amercameca, Estado de
Mexico*

Cornelio Flores A.
Amercameca, Edo. Mexico
*Trabajo en Kelowna y me gusta lo que hago en
Canada. Quisiera que todos los mexicanos que
venimos a Canada demos el esfuerzo siempre para
trabajar.*

Cornelio Flores A.
Amercameca, Mexico State
I work in Kelowna and I like what I do in
Canada. I would like that all the Mexicans that
come to Canada always have the strength to
work.

117. Everardo Demecio Sanchez Romero

Everardo Demecio Sanchez Romero
Doy las gracias a los patrones de Canada para que
la produccion rinda mas es echandole ganas a la
chamba y tengan mas empleo y asi mi familia tenga la
oportunidad de venir a conocer el trabajo y pueda llo
que mi economia rinda mas.

Everardo Demecio Sanchez Romero
I give thanks to the bosses of Canada for a
profitable production that makes one want
to work and that they would have more
employment, and so that my family has the
opportunity to come to know the work and that
my own finances may go further.

118. EDDY, Chiapas

*EDDY 2 años trabajo   Chiapas *agradecido con*
Dios por mi trabajo. D. T. B. (Dios Te Bendiga)

EDDY 2 years of work. Chiapas. *I thank God for
my work. God bless you.

119. Nelson Hernandez, Durango

Mi nombre es Nelson Hernandez Soy de Durango
Dgo
VIVE LA VIDA AL100%   NO LA DESPERDICIES
¡ANIMO!

My name is Nelson Hernandez. I'm from
Durango, Durango.
LIVE LIFE 100%. DON'T WASTE IT. COURAGE!

120. Daniel David Guido Páz, Uruapan, Michoacán

Daniel David Guido Páz   Michoacan — Uruapan
Estar tan lejos de tu pais te hace saber lo bonito que
(es) y no se diga sus festividades y costunbres y
grasias Canada por su apollo con el trabajo.

Daniel David Guido Páz   Michoacan — Uruapan
To be so far from your country makes you know
how beautiful it is, not to mention its festivities
and customs and thank you Canada for your
support with the work.

Because the pesticides on our skin are still glowing

Because

Introductory text to Deborah Koenker's Tortilla Wall photographs

By Juan Felipe Herrera, Poet Laureate of the United States

187

In 1994, I responded to the California Proposition 187, the 1994 ballot initiative. This was a state-run citizenship screening and prohibited undocumented persons ("illegal aliens") from using non-emergency health care, public education and other services in the state. Voters passed the proposed law as a referendum in late 1994. It was found unconstitutional by the federal court.

The number 187 seemed appropriate to write a list of reasons "why Mexicanos could not cross the border." My concerns had to do with the historical roots of Mexican@s and Latin@s in the USA as well as those related to corporate intrusion into Mexico and Latin America and a number of pop-cultural figures I thought would give the poem some "undocumented" spice. Most of all, I felt this proposed legislation overlooked all the contributions of Mexican@s and Latin@s that have helped shape and invigorate the economic, cultural and historical life of the state. The proposition lacked heart, compassion and socio-cultural knowledge.

Early Days

As a child of farmer workers, as a Campesino boy – I lived in a separate world from the typical, mainstream world of the 50s in California. Roads, mountains, ranchitos and the open landscapes of the San Joaquín Valley were my life. Skies and animals, my father's hand-made trailer, my mother's world of sayings, proverbs, corridos and stories about crossing into Juárez from Tepito, Mexico after the Mexican Revolution – these were the forceful currents that guided my young life. In my family, we went from extreme poverty in Mexico to just "plain ol' being poor" in the US. Later, after years of being a poet, and after many more being in the rise and fall of the Chican@ Movimiento, I became keenly aware that we really never were poor, we were enduring, incredible, and rock-hard pioneers. Poetry for me became much more than fancy words on paper – poems were beacons, speaker-comets that I could light-up and wave as I moved through streets, communities, and the cities of the nation.

The award-winning Juan Felipe Herrera grew up in California as the son of migrant farm workers. As well as having published more than a dozen collections of poems, he has written short stories and fiction for young adults. He was named poet laureate for California in 2012, and for the United States in 2015. The Kelowna Art Gallery and Deborah Koenker gratefully acknowledge Juan Felipe Herrera's American publisher, City Lights, in San Francisco, for making his work available.

187 REASONS MEXICANOS
CAN'T CROSS THE BORDER
(remix)

—Abutebaris modo subjunctivo denuo

Because Lou Dobbs has been misusing the subjunctive again

Because our suitcases are made with biodegradable maguey fibers

Because we still resemble La Malinche

Because multiplication is our favorite sport

Because we'll dig a tunnel to Seattle

Because Mexico needs us to keep the peso from sinking

Because the Berlin Wall is on the way through Veracruz

Because we just learned we are Huichol

Because someone made our ID's out of corn

Because our border thirst is insatiable

Because we're on peyote & Coca-Cola & Banamex

Because it's Indian land stolen from our mothers

Because we're too emotional when it comes to our mothers

Because we've been doing it for over five hundred years already

Because it's too easy to say "I am from here"

Because Latin American petrochemical juice flows first

Because what would we do in El Norte

Because Nahuatl, Mayan & Chicano will spread to Canada

Because Zedillo & Salinas & Fox are still on vacation

Because the World Bank needs our abuelita's account

Because the CIA trains better with brown targets

Because our accent is unable to hide U.S. colonialism

Because what will the Hispanik MBAs do

Because our voice resembles La Llorona's

Because we are still voting

Because the North is really South

Because we can read about it in an ethnic prison

Because Frida beat us to it

Because US & European Corporations would rather visit us first

Because environmental US industrial pollution suits our color

Because of a new form of Overnight Mayan Anarchy

Because there are enough farmworkers in California already

Because we're meant to usher a postmodern gloom into Mexico

Because Nabisco, Exxon, & Union Carbide gave us Mal de Ojo

Because every nacho chip can morph into a Mexican Wrestler

Because it's better to be rootless, unconscious, & rapeable

Because we're destined to have the "Go Back to Mexico" Blues

Because of Pancho Villa's hidden treasure in Chihuahua

Because of Bogart's hidden treasure in the Sierra Madre

Because we need more murals honoring our Indian Past

Because we are really dark French Creoles in a Cantínflas costume

Because of this Aztec reflex to sacrifice ourselves

Because we couldn't clean up hurricane Katrina

Because of this Spanish penchant to be polite and aggressive

Because we had a vision of Sor Juana in drag

Because we smell of Tamales soaked in Tequila

Because we got hooked listening to Indian Jazz in Chiapas

Because we're still waiting to be cosmic

Because our passport says we're out of date

Because our organ donor got lost in a Bingo game

Because we got to learn English first & get in line & pay a little fee

Because we're understanding & appreciative of our Capitalist neighbors

Because our 500-year penance was not severe enough

Because we're still running from La Migra

Because we're still kissing the Pope's hand

Because we're still practicing to be Franciscan priests

Because they told us to sit & meditate & chant "Nosotros los Pobres"

Because of the word "Revolución" & the words "Viva Zapata"

Because we rely more on brujas than lawyers

Because we never finished our Ph.D. in Total United Service

Because our identity got mixed up with passion

Because we have visions instead of televisions

Because our huaraches are made with Goodyear & Uniroyal

Because the pesticides on our skin are still glowing

Because it's too easy to say "American Citizen" in cholo

Because you can't shrink-wrap enchiladas

Because a Spy in Spanish sounds too much like "Es Pie" in English

Because our comadres are an International Political Party

Because we believe in The Big Chingazo Theory of the Universe

Because we're still holding our breath in the Presidential Palace in Mexico City

Because every Mexican is a Living Theatre of Rebellion

Because Hollywood needs its subject matter in proper folkloric costume

Because the Grammys & iTunes are finally out in Spanish

Because the Right is writing an epic poem of apology for our proper edification

Because the Alamo really is pronounced "Alamadre"

Because the Mayan concept of zero means "U.S. Out of Mexico"

Because the oldest ceiba in Yucatán is prophetic

Because England is making plans

Because we can have Nicaragua, Honduras, & Panama anyway

Because 125 million Mexicans can be wrong

Because we'll smuggle an earthquake into New York

Because we'll organize like the Vietnamese in San José

Because we'll organize like the Mixtecos in Fresno

Because East L.A. is sinking

Because the Christian Coalition doesn't cater at César Chávez Parque

Because you can't make mace out of beans

Because the computers can't pronounce our names

Because the National Border Police are addicted to us

Because Africa will follow

Because we're still dressed in black rebozos

Because we might sing a corrido at any moment

Because our land grants are still up for grabs

Because our tattoos are indecipherable

Because people are hanging milagros on the 2,000 miles of border wire

Because we're locked into Magical Realism

Because Mexican dependence is a form of higher learning

Because making chilaquiles leads to plastic explosives

Because a simple Spanish Fly can mutate into a raging Bird Flu

Because we eat too many carbohydrates

Because we gave enough blood at the Smithfield Inc., slaughterhouse in Tar Heel, North Carolina

Because a quinceañera will ruin the concept of American virginity

Because huevos rancheros are now being served at Taco Bell as Wavoritos

Because every Mexican grito undermines English intonation

Because the President has a Mexican maid

Because the Vice President has a Mexican maid

Because it's Rosa López's fault O.J. Simpson was guilty

Because Banda music will take over the White House

Because Aztec sexual aberrations are still in practice

Because our starvation & squalor isn't as glamorous as Somalia's

Because agribusiness will whack us anyway

Because the information superhighway is not for Chevys & Impalas

Because white men are paranoid of Frida's mustache

Because the term "mariachi" comes from the word "cucarachi"

Because picking grapes is not a British tradition

Because they are still showing *Zoot Suit* in prisons

Because Richie Valens is alive in West Liberty, Iowa

Because ? & the Mysterians cried 97 tears not 96

Because Hoosgow, Riata and Rodeo are Juzgado, Riata and Rodeo

Because Jackson Hole, Wyoming, will blow as soon as we hit Oceanside

Because U.S. narco-business needs us in Nogales

Because the term "Mexican" comes from "Mexicanto"

Because Mexican queers crossed already

Because Mexican lesbians wear Ben Davis pants & sombreros de palma to work

Because VFW halls aren't built to serve cabeza con tripas

Because the National Guard are going international

Because we still bury our feria in the backyard

Because we don't have international broncas for profit

Because we are in love with our sister Rigoberta Menchú

Because California is on the verge of becoming California

Because the PRI is a family affair

Because we may start a television series called *No Chingues Conmigo*

Because we are too sweet & obedient & confused & (still) full of rage

Because the CIA needs us in a Third World State of mind

Because brown is the color of the future

Because we turned Welfare into El Huero Félix

Because we know what the Jews have been through

Because we know what the Blacks have been through

Because the Irish became the San Patricio Corps at the Battle of Churubusco

Because of our taste for Yiddish gospel raps & tardeadas & salsa limericks

Because El Sistema Nos La Pela

Because you can take the boy outta Mexico but not outta the Boycott

Because the Truckers, Arkies and Okies enjoy our telenovelas

Because we'd rather shop at the flea market than Macy's

Because pan dulce feels sexual, especially conchas & the elotes

Because we'll Xerox tamales in order to survive

Because we'll export salsa to Russia & call it "Pikushki"

Because cilantro aromas follow us wherever we go

Because we'll unionize & sing *De Colores*

Because A Day Without a Mexican is a day away

Because we're in touch with our Boricua camaradas

Because we are the continental majority

Because we'll build a sweat lodge in front of Bank of America

Because we should wait for further instructions from Televisa

Because 125 million Mexicanos are potential Chicanos

Because we'll take over the Organic Foods business with a molcajete

Because 2,000 miles of maquiladoras want to promote us

Because the next Olympics will commemorate the Mexico City massacre of 1968

Because there is an Aztec temple beneath our Nopales

Because we know how to pronounce all the Japanese corporations

Because the Comadre network is more accurate than CNN

Because the Death Squads are having a hard time with Caló

Because the mayor of San Diego likes salsa medium-picante

Because the Navy, Army, Marines like us topless in Tijuana

Because when we see red, white & blue we just see red

Because when we see the numbers 187 we still see red

Because we need to pay a little extra fee to the Border

Because Mexican Human Rights sounds too Mexican

Because Chrysler is putting out a lowrider

Because they found a lost Chicano tribe in Utah

Because harina white flour bag suits don't cut it at graduation

Because we'll switch from AT&T & MCI to Y-que, y-que

Because our hand signs aren't registered

Because Freddy Fender wasn't Baldomar Huerta's real name

Because "lotto" is another Chicano word for "pronto"

Because we won't nationalize a State of Immigrant Paranoia

Because the depression of the '30s was our fault

Because "xenophobia" is a politically correct term

Because we shoulda learned from the Chinese Exclusion Act of 1882

Because we shoulda listened to the Federal Immigration Laws of 1917, '21, '24 & '30

Because we lack a Nordic/Teutonic approach

Because Executive Order 9066 of 1942 shudda had us too

Because Operation Wetback took care of us in the '50's

Because Operation Clean Sweep picked up the loose ends in the '70s

Because one more operation will finish us off anyway

Because you can't deport 12 million migrantes in a Greyhound bus

Because we got this thing about walking out of everything

Because we have a heart that sings rancheras and feet that polka

187 Reasons Why Mexicanos Can't Cross the Border, 1994. Revised.

– Juan Felipe Herrera

Deborah Koenker
Tortilla Wall Works

Tortilla Wall: Pacific Ocean, Tijuana, México, 2008, ink jet print mounted on Sintra, 10 x 40 in. (25.4 x 101.6 cm)

Tortilla Wall: fruit vendor, Pacific Ocean, Tijuana, México, 2008, ink jet print mounted on Sintra, 10 x 40 in. (25.4 x 101.6 cm)

Tortilla Wall: Danger, Tijuana, México, 2008, ink jet print mounted on Sintra, 10 x 40 in. (25.4 x 101.6 cm).

Tortilla Wall: La Migra (Immigration Patrol), Tijuana, México, 2008, ink jet print mounted on Sintra, 10 x 40 in. (25.4 x 101.6 cm).

Tortilla Wall: border mansion, Tijuana, México, 2008, ink jet print mounted on Sintra, 10 x 40 in. (25.4 x 101.6 cm).

Tortilla Wall: view north to San Diego, Tijuana, México, 2008, ink jet print mounted on Sintra, 10 x 40 in. (25.4 x 101.6 cm).

Tortilla Wall: Alberto, Tijuana, México, 2008, ink jet print mounted on Sintra, 13 x 30 in. (33 x 76.2 cm)

Tortilla Wall: Wall as corrugated snake, Tijuana, México, 2008, ink jet print mounted on Sintra, 10 x 40 in. (25.4 x 101.6 cm)

Tortilla Wall: The best bullfighters, Tijuana, México, 2008, ink jet print mounted on Sintra, 13 x 10 in. (33 x 25.4 cm)

Tortilla Wall: "Message to the Great Tenochtitlán" and slums, Tijuana, México, 2008, ink jet print mounted on Sintra, 10 x 40 in. (25.4 x 101.6 cm).

Tortilla Wall: American-deluxe Wall between Tijuana and Tecate, México, abandoned bus, Tijuana, México, 2008, ink jet print mounted on Sintra, 10 x 40 in. (25.4 x 101.6 cm).

Tortilla Wall: angry graffiti between Tijuana and Tecate, México, 2008, ink jet print mounted on Sintra, 10 x 40 in. (25.4 x 101.6 cm).

Tortilla Wall: desert between Tijuana and Tecate, México, 2008, ink jet print mounted on Sintra, 10 x 40 in. (25.4 x 101.6 cm)

Tortilla Wall: border town, Tecate, México, 2008, ink jet print mounted on Sintra, 10 x 26 in. (25.4 x 66 cm)

Tortilla Wall: The Great Wall, Tecate, México, 2008, ink jet print mounted on Sintra, 13 x 20 in. (33 x 50.8 cm)

Tortilla Wall: dead end street, Tecate, México, 2008, 10 x 40 in. (25.4 x 101.6 cm).

Tortilla Wall: rest stop, near Tecate, México, 2008, 13 x 10 in. (33 x 25.4 cm)

Tortilla Wall: Sonora Desert looking north to the USA, 2008, 10 x 26 in. (25.4 x 66 cm)

Tortilla Wall: Wall at Mexicali-Calexico border, 2008, 10 x 40 in. (25.4 x 101.6 cm)

Tortilla Wall: "Borderless," "Enough Dead," Mexicali, México, 2008, 10 x 40 in. (25.4 x 101.6 cm)

Tortilla Wall: "Capitalism is Death," "Not one more death," Mexicali, México, 2008, 10 x 40 in. (25.4 x 101.6 cm)

Tortilla Wall: "Go Back," "Wall of Shame," "Resist Colonialism," Mexicali, México, 2008, 10 x 40 in. (25.4 x 101.6 cm)

Tortilla Wall: two vicious perros, Mexicali, México, 2008, ink jet print mounted on Sintra, 13 x 10 in. (33 x 25.4 cm)

Tortilla Wall: Wall of water, Mexicali, México, 2008, ink jet print mounted on Sintra, 10 x 26 in. (25.4 x 66 cm).

Tortilla Wall: headed north, border crossing at Mexicali-Calexico, 2008, ink jet print mounted on Sintra, 10 x 13 in. (25.4 x 33 cm)

Dear Eater

As you bite into the crisp, juicy flesh of a Braeburn apple and enjoy its sweet tart flavour, or nibble on the soft, smooth texture of a large maroon-coloured Bing cherry with its burst of delicious sweetness, do you wonder about the invisible stories and networks that bring these marvellous fruits to your table? I do. I often think about the origins of the food I eat, the country of its origin, how it was grown and the agricultural traditions that attend my daily sustenance.

I don't know about you, but my childhood home and the media culture that surrounded it offered little understanding of the food system. Admittedly my father did own two fast food restaurants so perhaps something was bred in the bone, or more aptly, the gut, of my digestive and social imaginary. Unfortunately, though, this formative exposure offered no real sustenance or provisions. Meanwhile I think about food a lot, I cogitate on the practices – old, new and emergent – that inform its cultivation. Of course this isn't just about food. An apple isn't just an apple or a cherry a cherry, but mythic, textual, technical, political icons[1]; they are signs and symbols of food (in)justice. Through a kind of worlding brought on by social media, gourmet and 'whole food' culture (never mind issues of food security) I find myself wondering about the often hidden forces that make up the ever-unfolding global food system. I use the word worlding as a verb to suggest something that is ongoing and hopefully generative, a mediation and exploration on world building that might reference multiple origins, boundaries, ethnicities, governance, and even consciousness itself.[2] This constantly shifting and evolving worldview opens up thought-provoking conversations that inform consumer choices and reveal undisclosed realities, which in turn constitute every bite of the food we eat.

There is so much of the information I have gathered that I want to share: the dynamic hallucinatory musings inspired by the noonday sun and the marigold tea I have been drinking of late. I definitely feel some of their spectral effects; a sense that the apple sitting on the table in front of me, and the forces that gave it life, have travelled across space and through time.

In British Columbia I am blessed with a cornucopia of fresh produce from the Lower Mainland and the Okanagan, to name but two of the many nearby agricultural zones. Canada is the fifth-largest agricultural exporter in the world, and the price of food has continually risen for fresh fruits and vegetables– forty per cent since 1980. The 'costs' for this include the ever-increasing profit margin, expensive industrial processes, 'inexpensive' labour and gas-guzzling networks of distribution across the country and further afield. But I wonder what is the real cost of food, not for our wallets, but for the lives and cultures of those who work the soil and harvest the produce?

The North American Free Trade Agreement (NAFTA), which came into effect in 1994, had a profound impact on the Mexican economy and the lives of Mexican people. The value of Mexican-grown crops was diminished by imported and often subsidized Canadian and American produce, forcing millions of Mexican farmers off the land and away from their subsistence agricultural traditions. Not to mention the predatory practices engaged by companies like Monsanto in introducing genetically modified (GM) corn. As a result, Mexican farmers have had to make their livelihood elsewhere. Many went to the United States; others came further north to Canada through guest employment programs like the Seasonal Agricultural Worker's Program (SAWP). And yet despite their reliable, skilled work and contribution to the BC economy they are compensated with low wages, often less than the legal minimum, no overtime, and limited access to the services that they pay into. And they are subjected to paycheck deductions for social benefits such as Employment Insurance and the Canadian Pension Plan that they can never receive because of their "temporary" status.[3]

Consider the Okanagan Valley in Canada's most western province as a case study – it is a hub of fruit growing and winemaking where the agricultural industry depends on the employment of temporary migrant workers, many of whom are from Mexico. Not a new phenomenon, racialized labour practices in the Okanagan Valley have been part of this industry since colonization by the British in the 1880s; farm labour has been performed by First Nations people after their own experiences of dislocation from their land,

the Chinese, the Doukhobors, the Japanese, the Portuguese, French Canadians, and more recently Mexicans. NAFTA's signed agreements among North American governments (those of Canada, Mexico, and the United States) have provided Canada with newer markets for exporting Canadian products, as well as greater ease importing agricultural workers on a seasonal basis. This is seldom a fair exchange when the workers were pushed off their land back home and must travel thousands of miles north for their livelihood. And here in Canada they often have to deal with workplace abuse, housing challenges, geographic and linguistic isolation, as well as the possibility that they could be dismissed and deported by their sponsor for virtually any reason and without recourse.

With all these hardships I keep coming back to two questions: why do Mexican migrant farmers continue to come to Canada when the conditions and profits are so low? And what keeps them connected to their country and the families that must stay behind? The answer to the first is quite simply a lack of other employment opportunities, a lack of options, a lack of choice. The second question is harder to answer. In part they are willing to endure the sacrifices they make because of loyalty and dedication to the loved ones left behind. I speculate that this is further sustained by the traditions and histories of a culture suffused with religious, spiritual and vernacular imagery, not to mention inspiring stories that connect people across space and time.

For many Mexicans, the figure of the Virgin of Guadalupe, or *Nuestra Señora de Guadalupe*, binds the nation like no other. Prayers to her for protection are made with the belief that she intercedes in the common welfare of her supplicants. Her provenance goes back to an Aztec farmer named Juan Diego, also known as Juan Diegotzil (1474–1548). Back in the early sixteenth century, he was walking through Tepayac hill country north of Mexico City, a sacred site of the Aztec moon goddess, where he encountered an apparition of a beautiful woman radiating light. She revealed herself as the Virgin Mary and stated, "I desire a church in this place where your people may experience my compassion. All those who sincerely ask my help in their work and in their sorrows will know my Mother's Heart in this place. Here I will see their tears; I will console them and they will be at peace. So run now to Tenochtitlan and tell the Bishop all that you have seen and heard."[4] After much back and forth between Juan Diego and Bishop Fray Juan de Zumarraga, with three more visitations, a near death experience, a sign from the Virgin, and a mistranslation of the Aztec word *Coatlallope*, [5] the venerated icon of the Virgin of Guadalupe was born. Also known as Tonantzin, Our Sacred Mother in the Nahuatl language, she is the female Aztec deity symbolically connected to fertility and the earth. It is no wonder that migrant labourers have a special relationship to Guadalupe/ Coatlallope/Tonantzin, not only for her protection and her indigenous connections, but also because it was a farmer who received her visitation. And of course there is this divine figure's association with the solar cycle and with fertility.

The image of the Virgin of Guadalupe is recognized for its diverse and rich symbolism. The burst of the sun's rays around her figure speaks to Huitzilopochtli, the highest god in the Aztec pantheon, the Christian divine, and, I envision, the sowing and reaping of the harvest. The sunburst encircling her form evokes the warmth of Middle America, the solar energy of which generates the photosynthesis that feeds the plants and produces abundant crops. Where the sun shines in such abundance, fecundity is not far behind. I have even heard people suggest that the sun motif in this popular icon resembles the Labia Majora, and the virgin's robes, the darker folds of the Labia Minora, with her crowned head as the clitoris. This chimeric vision offers something of the fertile nature of Guadalupe/Coatlallope/Tonantzin, further linking her to agricultural productivity and bountiful labour. A vision of divine hallucination, the sun-kissed Virgin of Guadalupe is over-coded with meaning across time and Latino/a cultures, but its figuration is always connected to the earth and to female attributes.

Perhaps Cesar Chavez (1927-1993) and Dolores Huerta (born 1930) received their own inspired intercessions. Like Juan Diego, César Estrada Chávez was a farmer who had a vision. He was a Mexican American farm worker, who, with Dolores Huerta, co-founded the National Farm Workers Association (later the United Farm Workers Union). Throughout his career as a labour leader and civil rights activist, the work of Chavez brought significant improvements to farm workers and unionized labour. Like revolutionaries before him, for example Pancho Villa and Emiliano Zapata, Chavez employed the image of the Virgin of Guadalupe in rallying farm workers.[6] As an historical icon for the Latino/a community, Guadalupe has represented the rights of oppressed workers, moral commitment, and social justice. And Mexican-American Dolores Clara Fernández Huerta, in addition to her work as a labour leader and civil rights activist, has done much advocacy for the rights of worker,

immigrants, and women. Facing criticism based on both gender and ethnic stereotypes, Huerta along with Chavez, represents liberation and action to many in the Latino/a community, and by proxy both are also figures of abundance.

As with the Virgin of Guadalupe, there are other symbols that reflect the longevity and solar energy of Mexican culture. Take the marigold flower, a wild plant, harvested and used in spiritual and political offerings such as in the Day of the Dead celebrations, and cultivated for medicinal uses in its calendula varietal. Cempoalxochitl is the Nauhatl (Aztec) name, while horticulturalists gave it the Latin name *Tagetes erecta*. Its more potent form is called *Tagetes lucida*. Since Pre-Columbian times this flower has possessed magical properties used for divination and ceremonial purposes. It has been smoked as a rite of passage in sexual shamanic rituals, most likely due to its aphrodisiac effects. And in combination with other sacred ingredients it is said to produce hallucinations and dream enhancement.[7] Its name in English, Mary's Gold, refers to the Virgin Mary.

Sunlight, agriculture, and the farming traditions that have evolved around the Marigold invoke a magical power, a prayer, a blessing. On a daily basis, I am reminded of the powerful energy of sunshine as I enjoy the endless bounty and fruits of farm labor everywhere. I began this letter referring to worlding as part of our social imaginary, employed to encourage an ongoing exploration of possible worlds, different worlds. Still sitting here with a warm cup of Marigold tea, I find myself delving into many realms of experience – embodied and phantasmal – moving back-and-forth across time, but also between reality and representation. I believe that worlding and the possibilities it engenders are luminous. It is the world we inherit, the world we inhabit, and the world we eat. Whether an apple, a cherry, or the vast array of agricultural produce harvested near and far, these cultivated foods hold and absorb the traditions, histories and (in)justices of their manufacture, entangling the nascent affects of fertile imagery, common welfare, and an enduring solar energy.

Yours truly, Randy Lee Cutler

Endnotes
1. I borrow these adjectives from Donna Haraway's essay, "The Promises of Monsters: A Regenerative Politics for Inappropriate/d Others," Lawrence Grossberg, Cary Nelson, Paula A. Treichler, eds., *Cultural Studies* (New York; Routledge, 1992), pp. 295-337.
2. Martin Heidegger popularized the neologism in his 1927 book *Being and Time* to mean "being-in-the-world." http://worlding.org/what-in-the-world-2/
3. http://www.watershedsentinel.ca/content/seasonal-agricultural-workers-program-swap
4. http://www.catholic.org/about/guadalupe.php
5. Coatlallope has been translated as one who treads on snakes.
6. Roger Bruns, *Encyclopedia of Cesar Chavez: The Farm Workers' Fight for Rights and Justice*, Westport: Greenwood, 2013, p. 260.
7. (Siegel et al. 1977) http://entheology.com/plants/tagetes-lucida-marigolds/

Whether through performance art, experimental video, photographs, recipes, interventions, or critical writing, Randy Lee Cutler's practice explores the aesthetics of appetite, agency and embodiment. She contributes essays to catalogues and art magazines while maintaining an experimental relationship to pedagogy and gardening. Randy is an associate professor at Emily Carr University in the Faculty of Visual Art + Material Practice. *Open Wide: An Abecedarium for the Great Digestive System*, her ebook on digestion as a metaphor for experience, is available on iTunes.

Deborah Koenker, *Decorated grave, Day of the Dead, Oaxaca*, 2013.

121. *Diego Vizcarra Sanchez, Mazatlán, Sinoloa*

Mazatlán, Sinoloa Mexico
Mexico/Canada
Primera vez que vengo a Canada y espero regresar el
proximo año ya que si me gusto.
Diego Vizcarra Sanchez

Mazatlán, Sinoloa Mexico
Mexico/Canada
First time that I come to Canada and I hope to
come back next year, because I liked it.
Diego Vizcarra Sanchez

122. *Remigio Gonzalez, Yucatán*
Mi nombre es Remigio Gonzalez del estado de Yucatan
Es un gusto serbirle a Canada de cierta manera
al darme la oportunidad en trabajar para sacar en
adelante a mi familia. Viva Canada. Grasias.

My name is Remigio Gonzalez from the state
of Yucatan. It is a pleasure to serve Canada in a
certain way to give me the opportunity to work
to pull my family forward. Viva Canada. Thank
you.

123. *Fausto Ramirez, Estado de Mexico*

Fausto Ramirez   Estado Mexico
Tengo 6 años viniendo a trabajar en Canada e estado
en diferentes trabajos y me siento muy feliz por que
con el trabajo que estoy cosechando estoy sacando
adelante a mis hijos en el estudio, es muy bonito
Canada.

I have 6 years coming to work in Canada and I
have been in different jobs and I feel very happy
because with the work that I am harvesting I am
pulling forward my children in their studies.
Canada is very nice.

124. *Pablo Palma Contreras, Morelos*

Pablo Palma Contreras   Soy de Morelos
Mi pensamiento es que aqui gracias a Dios é hecho
dinero echandole ganas pero lejos de mi Familia
esperemos regresar bien para volver Pronto.

My thought is that here thanks to God I have
made money with a good effort but far from my
family. I hope to go back well and to return soon.

118

125. J. Antonio Cortes, Apazingán, Michoacán

J. Antonio Cortes
Soy de Apazingan Michoacan
Y vengo a Canada a trabajar por una major vida.

J. Antonio Cortes
I'm from Apazingan, Michoacan
And I come to Canada to work for a better life.

126. Markoz B. G., San Luis Postosi

Markoz B. G.   San Luis Postosi, Mx.
Trabajando todo los dias p' sacar p la "tortilla"

Markoz B. G.   San Luis Potosi, Mx.
Working everyday to get "the tortilla"

127. Raul Lechuga Ch, La Cruz, Chihuahua
Raul Lechuga Ch
Chihuahua La Cruz
Buena Temporada

Raul Lechuga Ch
La Cruz, Chihuahua
A good season.

128. Juan Francisco Hernandez Aguirre, Monterrey,
Nuevo León
Juan Francisco Hernandez Aguirre
Monterrey, N.L.
Es muy bonito Canada y la experiencia es que volveria
a venir.

Juan Francisco Hernandez Aguirre
Monterrey, Nuevo Leon
Canada is very nice, and the experience is such
that I would come back.

120

129. *Pedro Verduzco, Los Mochis, Sinaloa*

Pedro Verduzco
(Los Mochis, Sinaloa)
No somos violadores ni rateros como dice Trumph.
Somos trabajadores.

Pedro Verduzco
(Los Mochis, Sinaloa)
We aren't rapists or robbers as Trump says. We
are workers.

130. *José Gomez, Sonora*

*Soy Jose Gomez. Vengo del Estado de Sonora. A sido
una experiencia bonita al venir a este pais a trabajar.
Gracias Canada….. ☺*

I'm Jose Gomez. I come from the state of Sonora.
It has been a nice experience to come to this
country to work. Thanks Canada…. ☺

131. *Pedro Mendoza García, Zamora, Michoacán*

Pedro Mendoza Garcia
Zamora Michoacán
Mui Felis ☺

Pedro Mendoza Garcia
Zamora Michoacán
Very Happy ☺

132. *Eleuterio Cepeda Hernandez, Antiguo Morelos,
Tamaulipas*

Eleuterio Cepeda Hernandez
Antiguo Morelos, Tamaulipas, Mexico

Eleuterio Cepeola Hernandez
Antiguo Morelos, Tamaulipas, Mexico

133. Pedro Carona Carcaño, Tlaxcala

Pedro Carona Carcaño
Tlaxcala
mu bueno

Pedro Carona Carcaño
Tlaxcala
Very good.

134. Pablo Rodriguez Orduño, Ciudad Obregón, Sonora

Pablo Rodriguez Orduño
de Cd. Obregon, Sonora, Mexico
VIVO POR Y PARA MI FAMILIA POR SU
VIENESTAR LOS TENGO QUE DEJAR UNO
CUANTES MESES OK. GRACIAS C.

Pablo Rodriguez Orduño
de Ciudad Obregon, Sonora, Mexico
I LIVE FOR MY FAMILY FOR THEIR WELL
BEING . I HAVE TO LEAVE THEM FOR SOME
MONTHS, OK. THANK YOU C[ANADA]

135. Alejandro, Francisco I. Madero, Coahuila

Alejandro
Vive tu vida al maximo y disfrutala porque es corta.
Coahuila, Francisco I. Madero

Alejandro
Live your life to the maximum and enjoy it
because it is short.
Coahuila, Francisco I. Madero

136. Rafael Perez Rojas, Ayapango, Estado de México

Rafael Perez Rojas
Saves que Dios por eso asercate a Dios que te ama. E
de Mexico son de Ayapango.

Rafael Perez Rojas
You know God so be close to God that loves you.
State of Mexico, from Ayapango.

137. Juan Sanchez D., Hidalgo

Soy Juan Sanchez D. y soy del Edo. de Hidalgo.
Como trabajador Agricola me gustaria que el gobierno
Canadience me diera la oportunidad de traer a mi
Familia o que alguno de mis hijos viniera a estudiar en
este gran pais maravilloso.

I'm Juan Sanchez D. and I'm from the state of
Hidalgo.
As an agricultural worker I'd like that the
Canadian government give me the opportunity to
bring my family or that one of my children could
come to study in this great marvelous country.

138. "Eli" Garcia Hernandez, Chiapas, México

"Eli" Garcia Hernandez
Yo estoy aqui para trabajar por lo que mas quiero en la
vida: "Mi Familia"
Que Dios nos de las fuerzas a todos. Estado de
Chiapas, Mexic

"Eli" Garcia Hernandez
I am here to work for what I love most in life:
"My Family".
That God gives us all strength. State of Chiapas,
Mexico.

139. Andrés Noh U. C., Merida, Yucatán

Andres Noh U. C.
Gracias a Dios que me a dado la oportunidad de
trabajar aqui. De Merida, Yuc.

Andres Noh U. C.
Thanks to God that has given me the opportunity
to work here. From Merida, Yucatan.

140. Margaro Flores, Aticama, Nayarit

Recuerdo para mi Familia, Flores Garcia Los quiero
mucho
Margaro Flores. Aticama, Nayarit, Mexico

Regards to my Family, Flores Garcia. I love you
a lot.
Margaro Flores. Aticama, Nayarit, Mexico.

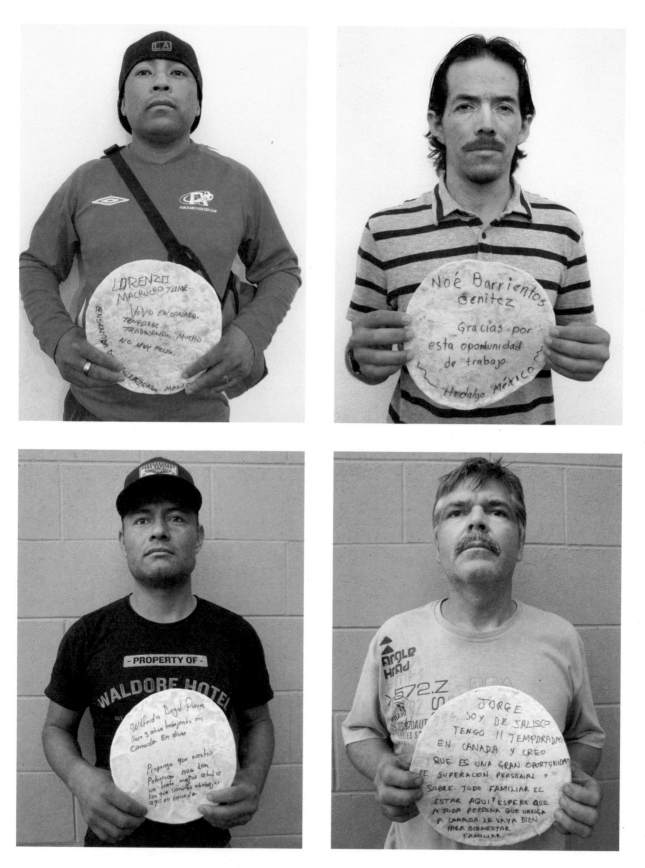

141. *Lorenzo Machucho Tome, Ensenada, Baja California*

Lorenzo Machucho Tome.
Vivo en Canada.
Tenporal.
Trabajando mucho.
No muy felix.
Ensenada, Baja California, Mexico

Lorenzo Machocho Tome
I live in Canada.
Temporarily.
I work a lot.
Not very happy.
Ensenada, Baja California, Mexico

142. *Noé Barrientos Benitez, Hidalgo*

Noé Barrientos Benitez
Gracias por esta oportunidad de trabajo
Hidalgo, México

Noé Barrientos Benitez
Thank you for this opportunity of work.
Hidalgo, México

143. *Wilfrido Angel Quiroz*

Wilfrido Angel Quiroz
llevo 3 años trabajando en Canada en Oliver
Propongo que nuestro Patrones nos den un trato
major a todos
los que venimos a trabajar aqui en Canada

Wilfrido Angel Quiroz
I have 3 years working in Canada in Oliver
I propose that our bosses give us a better
treatment to all
who come to work here in Canada

144. *Jorge, Jalisco*

Jorge
Soy de Jalisco
Tengo 11 temporadas en Canada y creo que es una
gran oportunidad de superacion personal y sobre todo
familiar el estar aqui y espero que a toda persona que
venga a Canada le vaya bien para bienestar familiar.

Jorge
I'm from Jalisco
I have 11 seasons in Canada and I believe it is a
grand opportunity of personal growth and for
the family, to be here and I hope that anyone who
comes to Canada does well for their family well
being.

145. *Juan Sanchez Martinez*

Juan Sanchez Martinez
Tengo 12 años viniendo a Canada
Espero que alguna vez venga a visitar mi Familia.
y que mi Familia algun dia venga a estudiar aqui en Canada
bonito pueblo de Oliver B.C.

Juan Sanchez Martinez
I have 12 years coming to Canada
I hope that some time my Family will come to visit.
and that my Family someday will come to study here in Canada
Pretty town of Oliver B.C.

146. *Amalio Hernandez Rodriguez*

Amalio Hernandez Rodriguez
Me gusta Canada y quisiera que alguien de my Familia algun dia vinieran porque es muy vonito este pueblo Oliver.

Amalio Hernandez Rodriguez
I like Canada and I would like that someone of my Family someday can come because it is very pretty this town of Oliver.

147. *Emiliano Garcia Juarez, Tlaxcala*

Emiliano Garcia Juarez
Tlaxcala   .
Extraño mi Familia querida

Emiliano Garcia Juarez
Tlaxcala
I miss my beloved Family.

148. *Efren Martinez Gonzalez, San Luis Potosi*

Efren Martinez Gonzalez de San Luis Potosi
Saludos a la familia Dahliwal y a mi familia en Mexico. Los extraño mucho.

Greetings to the Dahliwal family and to my family in Mexico. I miss them a lot.

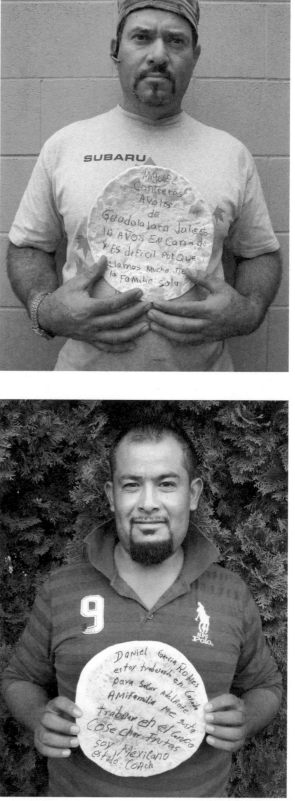

149. Guadalupe Roldán Rivera, Estado de México

J. Guadalupe Roldán Rivera del Edo de Mexico
Estoy muy contento de venir a Canada porque a mis
hijos les puedo ayudar en su educación
doy gracias a Dios al estar trabajando para Canada.

J. Guadalupe Roldán Rivera of the State of
Mexico
I'm very content to come to Canada because I can
help my children in their education. I give thanks
to God to be working for Canada.

150. Miguel Contreras Avalos, Guadalajara, Jalisco

Miguel Contreras Avalos de Guadalajara, Jalisco
10 años en Canada y es dificil porque dejamos mucho
tiempo la familia sola.

Miguel Contreras Avolos de Guadalajara, Jalisco
10 years in Canada and it is difficult because we
leave our family alone for a lot of time.

151. Juan Alejandro Alemán Avendaño, Linares,
Nuevo León

Juan Alejandro Alemán Avendaño
Linares, Nuevo Leon, Mexico
Tengo 9 temporadas trabajando en Canada
Orgulloso de ser Trabajdor Agricola
Trabajo para mi
Familia

Juan Alejandro Alemán Avendaño
Linares, Nuevo Leon, Mexico
I have 9 seasons working in Canada
Proud to be an Agricultural Worker
Working for my
Family

152. Daniel García Robles, Estado de Coachella

Daniel Garcia Robles
Estoy trabajando en Canada para sacar adelante
a mi Familia. Me gusta
trabajar en el canpo
cosechar Frutas
soy Mexicano estado Coach.

Daniel Garcia Robles
I am working in Canada to pull my family
forward.
I like to work in the fields cultivating fruits.
I'm Mexican, State of Coachella

153. Hipolit Pérez León, Amatenango de Valle, Chiapas

Hipolit Pérez León
Estoy trabajando en Canada para sacar adelante a mi familia. Tengo 3 temporadas
de estar veniendo aqui a Canada
Soy del Estado de Chiapas, mi pueblo se llama
Amatenango de Valle, Chiapas, Mexico.

Hipoit Pérez León
I'm working in Canada to pull my family forward. I have 3 seasons to be coming here to Canada.
I'm from the State of Chiapas, my town is called Amatenango de Valle, Chiapas, Mexico.

154. Irma Madrid Logo

Irma Madrid Logo
Tengo viniendo a Canada desde el 2000 asta 2015 mi vida a dependido de Canada por eso yo quiero a Canada y soy felis en Canada.

Irma Madrid Logo
I've been coming to Canada from 2000 to 2015 my life has depended on Canada therefore I love Canada and I'm happy in Canada.

155. Abelardo Estrada García, Miacatlán, Morelos

Abelardo Estrada Garcia
Miacatlan Morelos
Ten en mente que no solamente con profecion contribuyes al progreso de un pais.
Tambien de trabajador agricola
"si se puede"

Abelardo Estrada Garcia
Miacatlan Morelos
Keep in mind that it isn't only professions that contribute to the progress of a country.
It is also agricultural work.
"Yes you can"

156. Roberto Crispin Jimenez, Puebla

Roberto Crispin Jimenez
Puebla
Soy Mexicano y bengo a Canada a trab. x mi Familia
Grasias Canada

Roberto Crispin Jimenez
Puebla
I'm Mexican and I come to Canada to work for my family.
Thanks Canada.

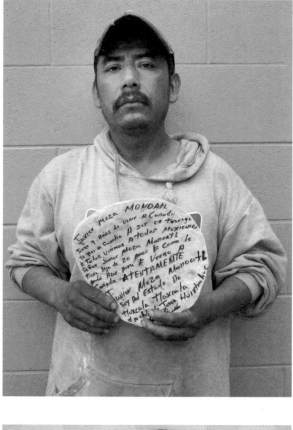

134

157. *Bernavé, Veracruz*

¡Hola! Soy Bernavé
y vengo de Veracruz
Llevo 4 años biniendo a Canada a trabajar
y la verdad es una oportunidad de trabajo para salir
adelante. Ojala y todos tubieran esta oportunidad.

Hi! I'm Bernavé
and I come from Veracruz
I've been coming to Canada for 4 years to
work and the truth is that this is a work
opportunity to move forward. I wish everybody
would have this opportunity.

158. *Javier Meza Manoatl, Jesús Huitznáhuac,*
Tlaxcala

Javier Meza Manoatl
Tengo 9 años de venir a Canada.
Yo por mi Familia a ser un travajo k todos
venimos a todos Mexicanos.
Señor Javier Meza Manoatl tiene hijo de
20 años. Como le puedo hzar para k
venga a Canada.
Atentamente
Javier Meza Manoatl
Yo soy del Estado de Tlaxcala
El pueblo de Jesús Huitznáhuac

Javier Meza Manoatl
I have 9 years coming to Canada.
I, for my family to be a work that everyone
comes, all the Mexicans.
Señor Javier Meza Manoatl has a son of
20 years. How can I help him to come to Canada.
Attentively
Javier Meza Manoatl
I am from the State of Tlaxcala
The town of Jesús Huitznáhuac

159. *Aurelio Silverio Gonzalez, Querétaro, Querétaro*

Aurelio Silverio Gonzalez
Soy de Queretaro, Queretaro. Animo paysanos ay
que seguir adelante para tener un futuro mejor para
nuestros hijos.

Aurelio Silverio Gonzales
I am from Queretaro, Queretaro. Courage
countrymen, we have to continue forward to
provide a better future for our children.

160. *Betty/Beatriz, Guadalajara, Jalisco*

Me parece un proyeto muy interesante para poder
concientizar a la sociedad Canadiénse aserca de los
Méxicanos
Betty

It seems to me a very interesting project to raise
awareness in Canadian society about Mexicans.
Betty

List of Works

Tortilla Portraits

There are 160 of these works in the exhibition, all dating from 2014 and 2015, and all printed as 21 x 16 inch (53.3 x 40.6 cm) inkjet prints.

Tortilla Wall Photographs

The exhibition includes twenty-five colour inkjet prints made from images created in 2008. The individual sizes are given with the image captions.

Additionally, several photographs (as inkjet prints) will be included by the artist, along with a selection of projected images, not listed at the time of publication printing.

The artist has also created installation pieces for the exhibition:

La Cocina (The Kitchen), 2016, mixed-media installation

Virgin of Guadalupe Shrine, 2016, mixed-media installation (orchard ladders, chairs, Loteria cards, votive candles, urns with marigold flowers)

La Frontera (The Border), 2016, vineyard netting with ribbons

Other works include:

Portrait of Sandy Diaz-Hart, Activist, 2015, inkjet print, 14 x11 in. (35.5 x 27.9 cm)

Interview with activist Doña Vicky, Oaxaca, 2013, audio recording in Spanish and English

Interview with Martín: account of crossing the Mexico-USA border, 2014, audio recording in Spanish and English

A musical soundtrack has been assembled by the artist to play in the gallery during the exhibition. The songs are by Lhasa de Sela, used with permission of the estate of Lhasa de Sela, and Lila Downs, used with permission of Cloud People Music.

Deborah Koenker

Selected Biography

Born

Chicago, Illinois, 1949

Education

1985	MFA (Sculpture / Installation), Claremont Graduate University, Claremont, California
1972-1973	Post-Grad, St Martins School of Art (now Central St. Martins), London, England
1971	BA/Fine Art (Drawing / Printmaking), University of California Santa Barbara

Professional Academic Experience

1992-2013	Associate Professor, Visual Art + Material Practice, Emily Carr University of Art & Design, Vancouver
1986-92	Sessional appointments in studio, Emily Carr Institute of Art & Design, Vancouver
1984-5	Teaching Assistant, Claremont Graduate University, Claremont, California
1983	Sessional appointment in studio, University of British Columbia, Vancouver
1981-4	Sessional appointments in studio, Emily Carr Institute of Art and Design, Vancouver

Selected Solo Exhibitions

2015	*Tela de Vidas*, Ayuntamiento de Gracia (Gracia City Hall), Barcelona, Spain, travelled to: Ciutat Vella, el Casal del Barri Pou de la Figuera, Barcelona, Spain and Universitat Rovira I Virgili, Tarragona, Spain

	Dibujando El Mundo: España (Drawing the World: Spain), Linea de Costa, Nave 5, ECCO, Cádiz, Spain
2008	*Deborah Koenker: Missing/Las Desaparecidas*, Richmond Art Gallery, Richmond, BC
	The Mexican Night, McGill Library, Burnaby, BC
2007	*Deborah Koenker: Ni Una Mas!/Not One More!*, Art Gallery, Rio Hondo College, Whittier, California
	Deborah Koenker: Missing/Las Desaparecidas, Guggenheim Gallery, Chapman University, Orange, California
	Deborah Koenker: Missing/Las Desaparecidas, Kathrin Cawein Gallery, Pacific University, Forest Grove, Oregon
	Deborah Koenker: Come To Your Senses, UICA (Urban Institute for Contemporary Art), Grand Rapids, Michigan
2006	*Deborah Koenker: Missing/Las Desaparacidas*, Galeria Manuel Felguerez, Universidad Autonoma Metropolitana, Mexico City, Mexico
	Deborah Koenker: Missing/Las Desaparacidas, Templo de San Antonio Centro Cultural, Tapalpa, Jalisco, Mexico

2004	*Deborah Koenker: Punctuation* print suite, permanent installation, Ithaca College Library, Ithaca, New York
2000	*Deborah Koenker: Adrift: a sculptural installation,* Richmond Art Gallery, Richmond, BC
1999	*Deborah Koenker: Adrift: a sculptural installation,* Open Space Gallery, Victoria, BC
1992	*Deborah Koenker: Bar-Ba-Loot: An Installation,* OR Gallery, Vancouver
1988	*Deborah Koenker: Learning from Salmon,* Contemporary Art Gallery, Vancouver
1986	*Deborah Koenker: Site-related Sculpture Installation,* Mendenhall Gallery, Whittier College, Whittier, California
1978	*Deborah Koenker: Pieces of Paper,* Artists Gallery, Vancouver, BC

Selected Group Exhibitions

2015	*Small Monuments to Food,* SkyTrain Canada Line kiosk, Lansdowne Station, Richmond, BC
	And they thought, where do we go from here?, 40th anniversary exhibition of the Malaspina Printmakers Founders, Malaspina Printmakers Gallery, Vancouver
2014	*Hard Twist: This is Personal,* Gladstone Hotel, Toronto
2011	*Sitely Premises,* Surrey Art Gallery, Surrey, BC
	Faculty Show, Concourse Gallery, Emily Carr University, Vancouver
2010	*More Than Flesh: embodiment of abstraction,* University of Toronto Art Centre, Toronto
	Faculty Show, Concourse Gallery, Emily Carr University, Vancouver
2009	*Recent Acquisitions,* Burnaby Art Gallery, Burnaby, BC
	Faculty Show, Concourse Gallery, Emily Carr University, Vancouver
2008	*Faculty Show,* Concourse Gallery, Emily Carr University, Vancouver
	Deborah Koenker: The Mexican Night, McGill Library, Burnaby, BC
2007	*Curriculum,* Malaspina Printmakers Gallery, Vancouver
	Faculty Show, Concourse Gallery, Emily Carr University, Vancouver
2006	*Tracking Absence,* A Space Gallery, Toronto

	Faculty Show, Charles H. Scott Gallery, Emily Carr University, Vancouver
2005	*Prints from Deer Lake,* Gallery at Ceperley House, Burnaby, BC
	25 Years+25 Artists, Richmond Art Gallery, Richmond, BC
	Prior Editions: 10 Years of Canadian Printmaking, Gallery at Ceperley House, Burnaby, BC, travelled to *The Works Festival,* Edmonton, Alberta
2004	*The Bookmark Project 2004: Interstate,* Koffler Gallery, Toronto
	A Graphic Eye, Art Gallery of Mississauga, Mississauga, Ontario
	Faculty Show, Charles H. Scott Gallery, Emily Carr University, Vancouver
2003	*Cutbacks,* Charles H. Scott Gallery, Emily Carr Institute of Art & Design, Vancouver
2002	*Oblique Obtuse Acute,* with Doug Biden, Gallery at Ceperley House, Burnaby, BC
	The Bookmark Project, FLEX site-works & interventions, Koffler Gallery, Toronto
	On Paper, University of Toronto Art Centre, Toronto
	Not Necessarily To Be Viewed As Art, Charles H. Scott Gallery, Emily Carr Institute, Vancouver
2001	*kicksART!,* The Roundhouse, Vancouver
	Prints from Canada's Pacific Province, Graphic Studio Gallery, Dublin, Ireland
2000	*Malaspina Printmakers: 25th Anniversary Exhibition,* Visual Arts Burnaby/Gallery at Ceperley House, Burnaby, BC
1999	*Path of a Body,* with Doug Biden, Alternator Gallery, Kelowna, BC
	Vancouver Vernacular, Charles H. Scott Gallery, Emily Carr Institute of Art & Design, Vancouver
1998	*Emily Carr Institute of Art & Design Invitational Print Exhibition,* in association with St. Petersburg State Academy of Art & Design, St. Petersburg, Russia
	Recent Acquisitions to the Permanent Collection Part II, Surrey Art Gallery, Surrey, BC
1997	*Heartfelt,* Prior Editions Ltd. Invitational Print Folio, Vancouver Art Gallery (sales and rental), Vancouver
1995	*Wall to Wall,* OR Gallery, Vancouver
1994	*Faculty Show,* Charles H. Scott Gallery, Emily Carr

Institute of Art & Design, Vancouver

1993   *Mary's Violet Eyes ...,* Artropolis 93: Surf & Turf,
        Stanley Park Site Work, Vancouver

        Faculty Show, Charles H. Scott Gallery, Emily Carr
        Institute of Art & Design, Vancouver

1992   *Faculty Show,* Charles H. Scott Gallery, Emily Carr
        Institute of Art & Design, Vancouver

1991   *Faculty Show,* Charles H. Scott Gallery, Emily Carr
        Institute of Art & Design, Vancouver

1990   *Within Range,* Prichard Art Gallery, University
        of Idaho, Moscow, Idaho (also Center for
        Contemporary Arts, Great Falls, Montana; Missoula
        Museum of Fine Arts, Missoula, Montana)

1989   *Works on Paper,* Charles H. Scott Gallery, Emily Carr
        Institute of Art & Design, Vancouver

        Dialogue: Deborah Koenker/Gary Geraths, Wignall
        Museum/Gallery, Chaffey Community College,
        Rancho Cucamonga, California

        Cactus – Mixed Emotions, The Art Works, Riverside,
        California

1987   *Riverside Collects: 5 Centuries of Graphic Art,*
        Riverside Art Museum, Riverside, California

        *The Cherry Tree Project: Site Specific Sculpture
        Collaboration* with Roberto Pacheco in three private
        gardens, Vancouver

        The Cherry Tree Project: Documentation, The
        Western Front, Vancouver

        Malaspina Printmakers Juried Members Show,
        Burnaby Art Gallery, Burnaby, BC

        Faculty Show, Charles H. Scott Gallery, Emily Carr
        College of Art & Design, Vancouver

1986   *Contemporary Prints: 35 Self-Portraits,* Claremont
        Graduate University, Claremont, California

1985   *MFA Exhibition,* East Gallery, Claremont Graduate
        University, Claremont, California

        U.C. Irvine Exchange, University of California Fine
        Arts Gallery, Irvine, California

        Ink and Clay XII, University Union Gallery,
        California State Polytechnic University, Pomona,
        California

        Parting Hot, Claremont Graduate University,
        Claremont, California

        Malaspina: Ten Years, Burnaby Art Gallery, Burnaby, BC

        *Malaspina Printmakers 10th Anniversary: Historical
        Show,* Burnaby Art Gallery, Burnaby, BC

1984   *Three from Vancouver,* Troisieme Galerie, Quebec
        City, Quebec

        Canada Council Art Bank Exhibition, Charles H.
        Scott Gallery, Emily Carr College of Art & Design,
        Vancouver

        Orange County Art Association, Brea Civic Cultural
        Center, Brea, California

1983   *Installation Art,* East Gallery, Claremont Graduate
        University, Claremont, California

        Deborah Koenker, Olga Froelich, Andy Petterson,
        Surrey Art Gallery, Surrey, BC

        Pacific Rim : Los Angeles Print Society, Beckstrand &
        Stewart Galleries, Rancho Palos Verdes,
        California

        Printmaking in British Columbia 1889-1983,
        Art Gallery of Greater Victoria, Victoria, BC,
        travelled to Confederation Centre Art Gallery,
        Charlottetown, PEI, and McIntosh Gallery,
        University of Western Ontario, London, Ontario

        Malaspina Printmakers Juried Members Show,
        Simon Fraser University, Burnaby, BC

        Recent Acquisitions, Burnaby Art Gallery, Burnaby, BC

        No U-Turn, Claremont Graduate University,
        Claremont, California

        *Gentle Interferences: Site Specific Sculpture
        Proposals,* Scripps College, Claremont,   California

1982   *Canada Council Art Bank Exhibition,* Charles H.
        Scott Gallery, Emily Carr College of Art & Design,
        Vancouver

        Malaspina Printmakers Juried Members Show,
        Robson Square Gallery, Vancouver

1981   *Faculty Drawing Show,* Charles H. Scott Gallery,
        Emily Carr College of Art & Design, Vancouver

        Malaspina Printmakers Juried Members Show,
        Robson Square Gallery, Vancouver

1980   *Members Drawing Exhibition,* Artists Gallery,
        Vancouver

1979   *Louis Crout, Diana Kemble, Deborah Koenker, Keith
        Mitchell,* Presentation House,   North Vancouver, BC

1978   *Handmade Paper: Extending the Process,* Vancouver
        Art Gallery, Vancouver, travelled to exhibition
        venues in Oliver, Nelson, Kaslo, Fernie, Invermere,
        Kamloops, Merritt, and Hope in British Columbia

        Malaspina Printmakers Juried Members Show,
        Burnaby Art Gallery, Burnaby, BC

1977 *Papier Systemes*, Optica Gallery, Montreal

Just Another Show, Pumps, Vancouver

1976 *Deborah Koenker/Judith Schwarz*, Artists Gallery, Vancouver, BC

Malaspina Printmakers, Centennial Museum Gallery, Langley, BC, and travelled through the province

1975 *Pacific Coast Consciousness*, Robert McLaughlin Gallery, Oshawa, Ontario, and travelled to Mount St Vincent University, Halifax, NS, Gallery/Stratford, Stratford, Ontario, Thames Theatre and Art Centre, Chatham, Ontario, London Regional Art Gallery, London, Ontario, University Gallery, University of Guelph, Ontario

Canadian Graphics Now, Contemporary Royale Gallery, Vancouver

The Provincial Collection, The Archives Gallery, The Provincial Museum, Victoria, BC

Malaspina Printmakers Juried Members Show, Paperworks Gallery, Vancouver

1974 *SCAN 1974: Survey of Canadian Art Now*, Vancouver Art Gallery, Vancouver, BC

ISIS: B.C. Women Artists, Women in Focus, Vancouver

1973 *Prints from St. Martins*, University of Sussex, Brighton, England

Publications by the Artist

"Deborah Koenker / Drawing the World/Le Monde," *The Capilano Review*, issue, 3, Vol. 22, 2014, pp. 107-113.

"Face to Face with Wanda Koop," *Wanda Koop: Face to Face*. Richmond: Richmond Art Gallery, 2009, pp. 51-60.

Observation of Wonder, Brenna Maag, exhibition brochure essay, Richmond: Richmond Art Gallery, 2009.

Missing/Las Desaparecidas, exhibition brochure essay. Richmond: Richmond Art Gallery, 2008.

"Thinking Textile," in *Craft Perception and Practice, Volume III*, Amy Gogarty and Nisse Gustafson, eds. Vancouver: Ronsdale Press, 2007, pp. 65-84.

Once Upon a Time, Frances Grafton, exhibition brochure essay, Richmond: Richmond Art Gallery, 2006.

Thinking Textile, Richmond: Richmond Art Gallery, 2003, pp. 4-35.

Adrift: a sculptural installation, artist's bookwork. Richmond: Richmond Art Gallery, 2000.

Dialogue: Deborah Koenker/Gary Geraths, Wignall Museum/Gallery, Chaffey Community College, Rancho Cucamonga, California, 1989.

"Doug Biden at Burnaby Art Gallery," *Vanguard,* November 1987, Vol. 16, no. 5, p. 32.

Related Professional Experience

2015 Co-founder with Karen Kazmer, Volcano Artist Collective, Vancouver

Public Art Commission, City of Richmond, BC

Artist in Residence, La Linea de la Costa, Cádiz, Spain

Artist in Residence, Jiwar, Barcelona, Spain

2011 Paris Studio, Canada Council International Residencies Program

2010 member of Public Art Selection Panel, Richmond, BC

2009 Guest Curator of *Wanda Koop: Face to Face*; Richmond Art Gallery, Richmond, BC

Guest Curator of *Ingrid Koenig: Navigating the Uncertainty Principle*; and *Brenna Maag: Observation of Wonder,* both for the Richmond Art Gallery, Richmond, BC

Member, Board Nomination Committee, Malaspina Printmakers Society, Vancouver

2005 Co-Curator of *Here and Away*, Malaspina Printmakers Gallery, Vancouver

Juror, Malaspina Printmakers Trilateral Exchange Exhibitions, Vancouver

2003 Artist's Residency, Atlin Art Centre, Atlin, BC

2002 Curator of *Thinking Textile* exhibition, Richmond Art Gallery, Richmond, BC

1999 Artist's Residency, Saskatchewan Writers Guild, St. Peter's Abbey, Muenster, Saskatchewan

1998 Artist's Residency, Dorland Mountain Artist Colony, Temecula, California

1995 Artist's Residency, Leighton Colony, Banff Centre, Banff, Alberta

1993 Jury member, Canada Council Project Grant

1976-1981 inaugural Director, Malaspina Printmakers Workshop, Vancouver

1975 Founding member, Malaspina Printmakers Society, Vancouver

Panels and Lectures

2009 Moderator for: Koop / Gu Xiong dialogue, Emily Carr University and Richmond Art Gallery, held at Emily Carr University of Art & Design, Vancouver

Panelist: *The Compulsion of Collecting*, Burnaby Art Gallery, Burnaby, BC

2007 Panelist: *Maquilapolis: Humans, Sweatshops and the Global Economy*, Pacific University, Forest Grove, Oregon

Panelist: *Missing/LasDesaparecidas*, Centro Cultural, Cornelius, Oregon

Panelist: *Women of Juarez*, Waltmar Theatre, Wilkinson College, Chapman University, Orange, California

Artist's Talk, Rio Hondo College, Whittier, California

2006 Presenter: *Missing and Taken: Symposium*, Dunlop Art Gallery, Regina Public Library & Dept. of Women's Studies, University of Regina, Regina, Saskatchewan

2000 Presenter, Peter Wall Institute Symposium: *Exploring Narratives of Disease, Disability, & Trauma*, University of British Columbia, Vancouver

Guest Lecturer, Rio Hondo College, Whittier, California

Panelist: *Invisible Disability: Personal, Political, Philosophical*, Richmond: Richmond Art Gallery, Richmond, BC

Artist's Talk, Open Space Gallery, Victoria, BC

1999 Guest Lecturer, Okanagan University College, Kelowna, BC

1999 Artist's Talk, Alternator Gallery, Kelowna, BC

1997 Guest Lecture, Malaspina Printmakers Society, Vancouver

Selected Awards

2014 Canada Council Project Grant

2011 Canada Council Paris Studio, International Residency Award

2008 British Columbia Arts Council Grant

2007 Canada Council Creation/Production Grant

2006 Canada Council Travel Grant

2004 British Columbia Arts Council Grant

2003 Canada Council Creation/Production Grant

2001 British Columbia Arts Council Grant

1998 Canada Council Project Grant

1997 British Columbia Arts Council Grant

1995 Canada Council Project Grant

1992 British Columbia Arts Council Grant

1989 Canada Council B Grant

1988 Canada Council B Grant

Canada Council Project Grant

1987 Canada Council Project Grant

1986 Finalist, US/Japan Artist Exchange Fellowship, National Endowment for the Arts

1985 Steele Foundation Fellowship

1984 Orange County Art Association Scholarship Award
Steele Foundation Fellowship

1983 Steele Foundation Fellowship

Canada Council Short-Term Grant

Canada Council B Grant

1981 Canada Council Travel Grant

1977 Honourable Mention: Malaspina Printmakers, Vancouver

1975 Local Initiative Projects, Artist's Grant, City of Vancouver

1974 Honourable Mention, Federation of Canadian Artists

1972 Manisphere International Scholarship Award, Graphics Award

Public Collections

Alberta College of Art & Design, Calgary, Alberta

Art Gallery of Algoma, Sault Ste. Marie, Ontario

Art Gallery of Greater Victoria, Victoria, BC

Art Gallery of Mississauga, Ontario

Banff Centre Library, Banff, Alberta

Burnaby Art Gallery, Burnaby, BC

Canada Council Art Bank, Ottawa, Ontario

City of Vancouver, British Columbia

Gallery Stratford, Stratford, Ontario

George Brown College, Toronto

Hope College, Holland, Michigan

Ithaca College, Ithaca, New York

Louisiana State University Museum of Art, Baton Rouge, Louisiana

Pacific University, Forest Grove, Oregon

Provincial Collection of British Columbia

Simon Fraser University, Burnaby, BC

Surrey Art Gallery, Surrey, BC

State University of New York at Buffalo, New York

University of Delaware, Newark, Delaware

University of Maine Museum of Art, Orono, Maine

University of Lethbridge, Lethbridge, Alberta

University of Toronto, Toronto

Vancouver Public Library, Vancouver

Corporate Collections

British Columbia Liquor Board

NaturoMed Health Clinic, Vancouver, BC

Portland Hotel, Vancouver, BC

Random House of Canada Limited

Security Pacific National Bank, N.Y., N.Y.

Toronto Dominion Bank

Selected Bibliography

Anon. "Mount offers a glimpse at our mysterious West," *Halifax Mail-Star,* January 26, 1976.

Anon. "La UAM rinde homenaje a las "muertas de Juárez"," *Cronica* (Mexico City), June 13, 2006.

Anzar, Nelda Judith. "Presenta Deborah Koenker en Tapalpa su exposición Las Desaparecidas," *La Journada Jalisco* (Jalisco, Mexico), August 3, 2006.

Anon. "Tras las huellas de los crimenes", *El Informador* (Mexico City), August 5, 2006.

Aguilar Garcia, Juan Carlos. "La UAM rinde homenaje a las "muertas de Juarez," *Cronica* (Mexico City), June 13, 2006.

Barrera, Laura. Live interview, Channel 22 Television, Mexico City, broadcast June 22, 2006.

Boulet, Roger. "Malaspina: Ten Years," *Newsprints* (Burnaby Art Gallery). Burnaby, B.C., September 1985.

Castellanos, Laura. "Pone Koenker rostro a victimas," *La Reforma* (Mexico City), June 9, 2006.

Castro Golarte, Laura. Live interview on Radio Metrópoli (Guadalajara, Jalisco, Mexico), August 1, 2006.

Ceballos, Miguel Angel. "Muertas de Juarez, la huella de una denuncia," *El Universal* (Mexico City), June 8, 2006.

Cline, Mary Alice. "*Riverside Collects: Five Centuries of Graphic Art,*" in Riverside Collects: Five Centuries of Graphic Art. Riverside, California: Riverside Art Museum, 1987.

Columbo, Flavia. "Las Desaparecidas/Missing," CNN Radio Espanol, Atlanta, Georgia, broadcast September, 2007

Dykk, Lloyd. "Junk art sizzles and hums with energy," *Vancouver Sun*, March 18, 1983.

Frater, Sally. "Tracking Absence", in *Tracking Absence: Deborah Koenker, Mae Leong, Femke van Delft, Charlene Vickers.* Toronto: A Space Gallery, 2006.

Fortes, Elizabeth. "Deborah Koenker/Roberto Pacheco: The Cherry Tree Project," broadcast on CBC Radio Brazil, April, 1987.

Godley, Elizabeth. "Unusual Sculpture Blossoms from Love of Cherry Tree", *Vancouver Sun*, April 10, 1987.

_____. "Fun title provides a fun exhibit", *Vancouver Sun*, March 23, 1988.

_____. "Paper Works More Relaxed", *Vancouver Sun*, March 2, 1989.

Hernandez, Sandra. "Desaparecidas," Universidad Autonoma Metropolitana (UAM) Radio Educacio, Mexico D.F., June 12, 2006.

Hoekstra, Matthew. "Violence Beyond Borders," The *Richmond Review*, May 1, 2008.

Keziere, Russell. "Malaspina Printmakers at the Burnaby Art Gallery", Arts Review on CBC Radio, May 25, 1978.

_____. "Deborah Koenker and Roberto Pacheco," *Vanguard*, November, 1987, Vol. 16, No. 5, pp. 33-34.

Laurence, Robin. "Stitching Out A Story," *The Georgia Straight*, December 4-11, 2003.

_____. "Missing traces violence against the vulnerable," *The Georgia Straight,* April 24, 2008.

Lynch, Sheila. Untitled text in *Deborah Koenker: Bar-ba-loot: an installation*, exhibition brochure essay. Vancouver: OR Gallery, 1992.

MacKay, Sheryl. "Thinking Textile," *North by Northwest* program, CBC Radio, December 28, 2003.

MacKillop, Michael-Scott. "Eleven artists displayed," *The Westender* (Vancouver), January 15, 1981.

McCallum, Paddy. "Representations of the Body Politic in the Art of Deborah Koenker and Doug Biden" in *Oblique Obtuse Acute*. Burnaby: Gallery at Ceperley House, 2002

Manzanera, Silvia. "El projecte col laboratiu de Jiwar es reforça amb l'exposició 'Tela de vides,'" *l'independent de Gracia* (Barcelona, Spain), April 30, 2015.

Martin, Aurora. "Tras las huellas de los crimenes," *El Informador* (Guadalajara, Jalisco, Mexico), August 5, 2006.

Martinez, Anzar and Judith Nelda. "Presenta Deborah Koenker en Tapalpa su exposicion *Las Desaparecidas*," *La Journada Jalisco* (Guadalajara, Jalisco, Mexico), August 3, 2006.

Matzkuhn, Bettina. "Thinking Textile," *ARTichoke*, Vol. 16, Summer, 2004, pp. 30-33.

Olvera Barragan, Estrella. "Desaparecidas: presencia tangible de las muertas de Juarez," *Semanario de La UAM* (Mexico City), June 12, 2006.

Perez Canedo, Adriana. Live interview, Channel 11 Television, Mexico City, June 12, 2006.

Rosenberg, Ann. "Dr Seuss tale inspires Deborah Koenker's Bar-Ba-Loot at the OR Gallery," *Vancouver Sun*, September 26, 1992.

Ryley, Bryan. "Making Paper," *Vanguard,* Vol. 7, No. 2, March, 1978, p. 19.

Sandals, Leah. "Sitely Premises: The Backyard as Studio," posted on *Canadian Art* online, 2011.

Talve, Merike. *Learning from Salmon*. Vancouver: Contemporary Art Gallery, 1988.

Tuele, Nicholas, Leslie Dawn, Leslie and Greg Bellerby. *Printmaking in British Columbia,* 1889-1983. Victoria: Art Gallery of Greater Victoria, 1983.

Velasco, Edgar. Article in *El Publico* (Guadalajara, Jalisco, Mexico), August 5, 2006.

Wilson, Peter. "Artropolis Putting Art in its Place," *Vancouver Sun*, October 30, 1993.

Wood, Alan. "Artropolis 93 is up on the issues," *Vancouver Sun,* October 30, 1993.

Zwicky, Jan. "Deborah Koenker Adrift: A Sculptural Installation," *Lola* magazine, Spring, 1999.

Artist's Acknowledgements

There are many to thank and acknowledge in the process of producing this exhibition. First and foremost, I thank all the Mexican seasonal agricultural workers toiling in the Okanagan Valley and across Canada, for the food that we eat and the wine that we drink, and for their love and dedication to the families left behind in Mexico. Special thanks to those men and women who participated in this project, so openly and graciously, trusting me with their words and their images, and to Doña Vicky, of Oaxaca, and Martín, of Michoacán, for their informative and moving interviews. *Un agradecimiento especial a los hombres y mujeres que participaron en este proyecto tan abierta y amablemente, por confiar en mí con sus palabras y sus imágenes.*

I am deeply grateful to the Kelowna Art Gallery and its staff for the opportunity to present this work, especially for the preparatorial assistance and the catalogue design. Very special thanks to Liz Wylie, Curator, for her early support and recognition of the importance of this subject, and for her excellent essay on my practice; also for her vision, patience, professionalism, and dedicated work in bringing this exhibition and catalogue to fruition. It has been a pleasure to work with her.

I thank the distinguished writers – Randy Lee Cutler, Juan Felipe Herrera and John Vaillant – for their outstanding and insightful essays on the various aspects of this subject from their particular and informed perspectives. *¡Mil gracias a todos!* Thank you to the following for their generous assistance: Cloud People Music for permission to use songs by Lila Downs, the estate of Lhasa de Sela for permission to use her song *La Frontera*, the Digital Output Centre at Emily Carr University of Art and Design and the technical expertise of Carlos Mendez and Eduardo Rodriguez, The Flag Shop, Vancouver, for their support in producing the Virgin of Guadalupe hanging, Growers Supply, Kelowna, for the donation of vineyard netting, Laura Geen at Jealous Fruits for the loan of orchard ladders, Nora Blanck, Janice Ball, Frances Grafton, Karen Kazmer, Lynette Klein, and Ingrid Koenig for spirited assistance with tying ribbons, and gallery volunteers who have supplied fresh marigold flowers for the exhibition. Thanks to Jeremy Koenker for sound editing assistance, and to Paloma Pacheco for English translations for Spanish audio interviews. Grateful acknowledgement to Mara Marquez and Sandra Martínez of KIWO, Elise Hahn and Amy Cohen of RAMA (Radical Action with Migrants in Agriculture), and Jany Lopez of Jany Lopez Latin Foods, and unnamed others for their assistance to farm workers in the Okanagan Valley and to this project.

This exhibition would have been impossible without the support of the Canada Council for the Arts, and the British Columbia Arts Council, specifically for the production of *Tortilla Wall (2008).*

Curator's Acknowledgements

This project has been an exciting and inspiring one to be immersed in and I thank the artist Deborah Koenker for her vision and hard work at every turn. It has been a very positive experience to work with her and to spend time looking at the photographs she has made of the temporary Mexican agricultural workers in the Okanagan. So many of us who live here are not aware that these men and women are in our midst and are harvesting the fruits of this fertile region. We hope this exhibition will help in correcting this ignorance.

I extend my sincere thanks also to the writers in this publication – the US poet Laureate, Juan Felipe Herrera, the award-winning John Vaillant, and multi-talented university professor and artist, Randy Lee Cutler. I am deeply grateful for their time, research, and thinking both on this topic and about Deborah Koenker's work.

Thanks as always to the staff and Board of the Kelowna Art Gallery who make this a fun and supportive place to create exhibitions such as this one.

– Liz Wylie, Curator

Finally, huge recognition is in order to Sandy Diaz-Hart for her assistance in introducing me to the farm workers, for her ongoing advice in regard to this project, and for her continuous advocacy, support and assistance to farm workers in so many aspects of their lives in the Okanagan, both practical and spiritual. And to my partner, Roberto Pacheco, for his constant ongoing support of my work, and specifically for serving as ambassador and go-between, making it possible to connect with these workers. *Gracias y un grandísimo abrazo.*

– Deborah Koenker

DEBORAH KOENKER
Grapes and Tortillas

July 16 to October 30, 2016 at the Kelowna Art Gallery

 KELOWNA GALLERY

1315 Water Street, Kelowna, BC V1Y 9R3
t: 250.762.2226 | f: 250.762.9875
www.kelownaartgallery.com

Library and Archives Canada Cataloguing in Publication

Deborah Koenker : grapes and tortillas.

Catalogue of an exhibition held at the Kelowna Art Gallery from July 16
to October 30, 2016.
ISBN 978-1-896749-80-8 (paperback)

1. Koenker, Deborah--Exhibitions. I. Wylie, Liz, writer of added
commentary, organizer II. Koenker, Deborah. Works. Selections.
III. Kelowna Art Gallery, issuing body, host institution IV. Title: Grapes
and tortillas.

N6549.K58A4 2016   709.2   C2016-903459-3

 City of **Kelowna**

 **Canada Council
for the Arts**   **Conseil des Arts
du Canada**

 **BRITISH COLUMBIA
ARTS COUNCIL**
An agency of the Province of British Columbia

 **BRITISH
COLUMBIA**
The Best Place on Earth

The Kelowna Art Gallery gratefully acknowledges the financial assistance
of the City of Kelowna, The Canada Council for the Arts, British Columbia
Arts Council, the Province of British Columbia, Central Okanagan School
District #23, Regional District of Central Okanagan, Central Okanagan
Foundation, and our members, donors and sponsors. Special project
support provided by the Audain Foundation, Telus Community Fund,
and the Vancouver Foundation.

Catalogue design and exhibition photography by Kyle L. Poirier
Printed by

 wayside

 **RECYCLED**
Paper made from
recycled material
FSC   FSC® C012744
www.fsc.org

Cover image: Deborah Koenker, *Abelardo Estrada García, Miacatlán, Morelos* (detail), 2015, ink jet print, 21 x 16 in. (53.3 x 40.6 cm);
text in English: Keep in mind that it isn't only professions that contribute to the progress of a country. It is also agricultural work.
"Yes you can"